WOW!

Lynn's Menu Collection

By Lynn Wolter

Compiled with commentary
by Bill Wolter

Do not neglect hospitality, because through it some have
entertained angels without knowing it. Hebrews 13:2

DEDICATION

From Lynn: This book is dedicated to the Women of Wisdom (WOW) and the
volunteers that have served with me at Northshore Baptist Church, Kirkland, WA.

From Bill to Lynn, This Book is Dedicated to the One I Love.
(Does anyone remember, The Shirelles, 1959, "...Each night before I go to bed my
baby, WEEEEE-YUUUUU, etc."?)

CONTENTS

ACKNOWLEDGMENTS

This book was made possible by the Women's Ministry of Northshore Baptist Church in Kirkland, WA., by giving Lynn the venue to cater monthly luncheons for the Women of Wisdom (WOW), for which individual menus were created and none were repeated for 13 years. Service to the WOW is to honor the King of the Universe, Jesus the Christ.

SPECIAL THANK YOU

To Laveda Miles and Hilario Pardo for proof review contributions.

Introduction

This book is a **Menu Collection** that is designed to assist the:

Chef, Cook, Event Coordinator, Wedding Coordinator, Reception Coordinator or General Meal Planner, Host and Hostess and **Homemaker**.

Complete with the necessary recipes, it provides an efficient guide for complete meal planning. The research for what goes with what has already been done. The menus and recipes have been tried and tested and received great reviews by honored guests with numbers ranging from 2 or 3 to over 100. I am the very fortunate husband of a wife who might love me a little more than she loves preparing and presenting food. Most of the menus have been served by Lynn at monthly luncheons for the ladies of Northshore Baptist Church in Kirkland, Washington, (**www.nsb.org**). She has applied her special gift of hospitality to the ladies for over 13 years, still on-going.

Hand compiled recipe books

That whole idea would be cruel and unusual punishment to me.

It takes people like Lynn to feed the rest of us. Make this book your handbook, use it, apply the menus and recipes, enjoy the fun facts and anecdotes scattered throughout, and prepare to receive wonderful compliments from your company.

– Bill

P.S.
Many of you are going to ask, "What wine shall I serve?"

There are plenty of books on wine. This is not one of them.

All I'm going to say about that is this:
- Most every menu can be enjoyed with your favorite dry red or white wine, according to your preference.
- Try a good dry red (not blush) California Zinfandel. Vines have been in California since the 1800's. Opinion has the origin in Old World regions from Italy to Croatia.

Find Out: Who is Coming to Dinner?

To use this book, find something that appeals to your taste, follow the accompanying recipes and enjoy. But what about the guests? I remember a time when a guest gladly accepted a dinner invitation without qualifications. Now we have to listen to their food allergies and likes and dislikes, not only of themselves, but also of their siblings, relatives and friends who are afflicted with similar dysfunctional bodies. If that doesn't knock the joy out of entertaining, some foods are not acceptable due to a religion or season of fasting, and on and on, etc. Oh yea- "We can't wait to enjoy the meal and your company!"

Some people have peculiar idiosyncrasies related to food. One of my daughter's by my middle son's marriage will not eat anything that has an appearance reflecting its original state as a living creature. For example, if meat is served still on the bones, it will be turned down. Also, we have a friend who will not eat anything that has had a mother, including an egg. We can label her a vegetarian.

Sometimes the guest must bear the responsibility. We have a friend who carries a small shaker of powered habanero pepper. He can always satisfy his craving to catch his mouth on fire to the tune of about 350,000 Scoville units.

(To establish a reference point, Cayenne pepper ranges from 30-50,000 Scoville units. Habanero ranges from 100-350,000 Scoville units. The Scoville unit is a measure of degree of pungency of a pepper according to a scale developed by Wibur Scoville in 1912.)

That's enough about hot peppers. Our fathers would not eat them. Neither would they eat poultry. With everyone else, chicken is popular.

Here is a sweet story about a considerate guest. The lady had a severe food allergy. She would call Lynn before a luncheon to see if she could eat what was on the menu. If necessary, she brought a substitute dish for herself. Now that was a gracious guest!

As for me. food tastes fall into one of these categories:

- Ladies like soup and salad. About 90% of the ladies have an "eat slim" attitude, but will share a dessert. My guess is that soup and salad and sharing the dessert does not add to the calorie count.

- Men like meat, potatoes and dessert. Some will eat vegetables.

- Some people who are obsessed with their work eat from vending machines.

Where do Recipes Come From?

The answer is easy. They come from cookbooks. Lynn must have over a hundred of them in her library.

That's where the main ideas come from, but...

they get "refined" by Lynn's experimenting. One day I came home from work and walked in on Lynn in the kitchen flushing a whole chocolate cake down the garbage disposal. I was not used to this practice. (*Like tasting wine then spitting it out. What's wrong with it; wasn't it good enough to drink?*) Lynn was doing R&D (research and development) in the kitchen – a normal process for her hobby of trying out recipe variations. I'm getting used to her kitchen operations.

Lynn's family recipes have accumulated over three generations. Many recipes are compiled in manually hand-written notebooks, representing years of experimenting to refine recipes for a culture of good eating. Older entries were made by Lynn's late mother, Evelyn Hinkle Hemphill. Of course, Lynn's library is not lacking of many published books regarding food preparation. An avid collector of such manuscripts, books range from the original Fanny Farmer 1896 Cookbook from the Boston Cooking School, to famous chefs' signature books and reference books by institutions such as Gourmet and the New York Times. Contemporary hard and soft bounds are routinely added according to value of content. Many friends have gifted her with cookbooks that she treasures.

The Sources section at the end of this book refers to the idea originators of the listed recipes.

Now Lynn spends more time on designing menu content for various lunch, dinners and events requiring fine food.

As stated in the New York Times Cook Book, *"Cooking is one of the simplest and most gratifying of the arts, but to cook well one must love and respect food."*

In our house there exists a lot of love and respect, not only for the food, but also, for the hands that prepare it.

Home of many recipes in North Carolina

- Bill

ILLUSTRATIONS

Graphics are scattered throughout the book, all black and white, where all originals were in color. Except for a few clip-art bits that are available through *Microsoft Office*, the originals are photos that were taken by Bill Wolter or a family member. Some distorted pictures are photos processed to appear like pencil graphics. All five of our current grandchildren appear in at least one or more photos. Shain Rievley of Bloom Photography in Knoxville, TN, captured the young Miss Rievley and Miss Wolter having tea on page 55.

Abbreviations used in This Book

Gallon(s)	gal.
Ounce(s)	oz.
Pint(s)	pt.
Pound(s)	lb.
Quart(s)	qt.
Tablespoon(s)	Tbs.
Teaspoon(s)	tsp.

PROOF OF CONCEPT

The Start of Menu Planning

Lynn's menu-planning era began with this modest selection featuring chicken salad on a croissant. Having never catered a meal for a large number of guests (over 50), she wanted to serve something simple yet delicious, keeping in mind that it was to be a sit-down luncheon.

The First Menu

Chicken Salad on Croissant

CHICKEN SALAD CROISSANTS

FRESH BROCCOLI SALAD

FRESH FRUIT

BLUEBERRY CREAM CAKE

ITALIAN PAN ROLLS

The result was an overwhelming success. Now 13 years and over 100 luncheons later, it's time to enjoy some of the good food.

Dress up your chicken salad with a croissant!

PROOF OF CONCEPT

Chicken Salad Sandwich

Ingredients

4 cups cubed cooked chicken
¾ cup chopped pecans
1 cup sliced celery
⅔ cup mayonnaise
⅓ cup sour cream
2 tsp. Lemon juice
Salt & freshly ground pepper, to taste
Lettuce
Croissants

Instructions

Use leftover cooked chicken or cook whole chicken breasts in water to cover seasoned with 1 tsp. Salt, 5 peppercorns, and one small onion stuck with 2 cloves. Cook until tender, about 25-30 minutes. Cool, skin, and cut into nice big chunks. In large bowl, place the chicken, pecans, celery, grapes, apples, and pineapple. Stir together the mayonnaise, sour cream, lemon juice, and ample salt and pepper; add to chicken and mix gently so as not to break up chicken chunks. Serve on crisp lettuce leaves. Serves 6.
In this case, serve on a croissant!

I have used this method of preparing chicken salsd since 1984 and have not found a better one. It was given to me by Jimmy Allen, a friend who was a fellow expatriate in Saudi Arabia.

"I do not like broccoli. And I haven't liked it since I was a little kid and my mother made me eat it. And I'm President of the United States and I'm not going to eat any more broccoli.." –George H.W. Bush. (It's his loss.)

Fresh Broccoli Salad

Ingredients

1 bunch broccoli
1 head cauliflower
1 medium red onion
½ lb. bacon, crisp and crumbled
1 cup shredded cheddar cheese
Dressing
2-3 Tbs. red wine vinegar
¾ cup mayonnaise
¼ cup sugar
Add raisins, sunflower seeds, etc., to taste

Instructions

Cut cauliflower and broccoli into bite-size pieces. Slice onion into thin slices and separate. Fry bacon crisp and crumble. Mix vegetables, bacon and cheese. Pour dressing over vegetables and let stand at least one hour. Refrigerate. Serves 10-12.

Menu: Chicken Salad on Croissant

PROOF OF CONCEPT

Blueberry Cream Cake

Ingredients

½ lb. Butter
½ cup shortening
3 cups sugar
6 eggs
1 tsp. Vanilla
1 tsp. Lemon
3 cups sifted plain flour
½ tsp. Baking powder
pinch of salt
1 cup sweet milk

Topping:
1- 3½ oz. package
instant vanilla pudding mix
1 cup heavy or
whipping cream
1 tsp. almond extract
1 pt. blueberries

Instructions

About 3 hours before serving or early in the day: Preheat oven to 325F.

Cream butter, shortening and sugar until light and fluffy. Add vanilla and lemon and blend well. Add eggs, one at a time, and continue beating after each addition.Sift together flour, baking powder and salt and add alternately to creamed mixture with milk. Pour into a greased and floured good-sized tube pan. Bake in a 325 F. oven for 1 ½ hours or until cake tests done

Note: I often use almond flavoring in this recipe, (my family's favorite).

When cake is cool, in large bowl with mixer at low speed, beat milk and instant vanilla pudding mix until thickened, about 2 minutes. In small bowl, with mixer at medium speed, beat cream until stiff peaks form. Gently fold whipped cream and almond extract into pudding mixture.

Place cake, indented-side up, on dessert plate (if cake is baked in 9" by 9" baking pan, place cake top-side up). Spoon cream mixture onto top of cake; refrigerate until slightly firm, about 30 minutes. Pat blueberries on cream mixture. Refrigerate. Makes 10 servings.

.*Bundt flan pan is available from Northland Aluminum Products, Inc., Highway 7 at Beltline, Minneapolis, MN. 55416.

Menu: Chicken Salad on Croissant

PROOF OF CONCEPT

Italian Pan Rolls

Ingredients

1 cup warm water (105-115)
1 Tbs. sugar
1 pkg. (½ oz.) dry yeast
2 ¾ cup flour
1 Tbs. butter or margarine
1 tsp. garlic salt
½ tsp. Italian herb seasoning or
¼ tsp. each basil and oregano
2 Tbs. melted butter
¼ cup grated Parmesan cheese

Instructions

Combine ¼ cup of the water, sugar, and yeast. Stir to dissolve yeast and let stand until bubbly, about 5 minutes. Heat remaining water and butter together in pan just until butter melts. Cool to 105°F. to 115°F. Measure 2 cups flour, garlic salt, and herb seasoning into large bowl; mix well. Add cooled water/butter mixture and yeast mixture; beat until smooth. Mix in enough remaining flour to make dough easy to handle. Turn dough onto lightly floured board; knead until smooth and elastic, about 10 minutes. Place in greased bowl and turn greased side up. Cover loosely with plastic wrap and let stand in warm place (85°F.) about 30 minutes. Divide dough into quarters, and then divide again into quarters, making 16 pieces. Shape each piece into a ball, dip in butter, coat with cheese and arrange in greased 8 or 9-inch round or square cake pan. Cover loosely with plastic wrap. Let stand in warm place until doubled, 1-1 ½ hours. Heat over 375°F. Uncover rolls and bake until golden, about 25 minutes. Remove immediately from pan and cool on wire rack.

Menu: Chicken Salad on Croissant

BE MY VALENTINE

Valentine Menu

Ham and Red Pepper Quiche

Ham and Red Pepper Quiche

Spinach Salad with Strawberries

Cherries in the Snow

Pope Gelasius declared February 14 St. Valentine's Day at the end of the 5ᵗʰ century - about the time when the ides of February pagan holiday, Lupercalia, was outlawed as "un-Christian." Hallmark Cards wasn't established until 1910. That means that Valentine notes were home-made for about 1,400 years. I wonder what took Hallmark so long?

Be My Valentine,

Lynn.

- Love, Bill

BE MY VALENTINE

Ham and Red Pepper Quiche

Ingredients

¼ lb. cooked bacon cut in pieces
1 medium-size onion sautéed in
small amount of bacon fat
¼ tsp. Salt
¼ tsp. Pepper
4 eggs
1 cup milk
½ cup heavy cream
¼ cup Parmesan cheese
¼ cup Swiss cheese
½ tsp. dry mustard
⅛ tsp. cayenne pepper
Dash of nutmeg

Instructions

Place cooked bacon anad sauteed onion on bottom of pan.Blend all ingredients and pour into a pie shell. Bake at 350 for 20 minutes or until firm.

Note: Cooking time can be a bit longer, (35-45 minutes, depending on your oven). Also, I added 1 cup ham and ⅓ cup red pepper (sautéed with the onions). Red was the theme of the day.

Spinach Salad with Strawberries

Ingredients

1 ½ cups sugar
1 ½ tsp. paprika
¾ tsp. dry mustard
1 ½tsp. Worcestershire sauce
1 ½ cups oil
1 ½ tsp. minced onion
¾ cup vinegar
⅓ cup poppy seeds
⅓ cup sesame seeds, toasted
1 lb. spinach
1 pt. fresh strawberries, sliced
4 medium bananas, sliced
1 cup chopped walnuts

Instructions

Prepare dressing by combining sugar, paprika, mustard, Worcestershire, oil, onion, vinegar and seeds in a blender; process until well mixed. Layer torn spinach, fruits and nuts on plate and top with dressing. Serves 12.

From Uptown Down South

Cherries in the Snow

Ingredients

1 (8 oz.) soft tub of cream cheese
¾ cup sweet milk
1 (8 oz.) angel food cake
½ tsp. Almond flavoring
½ cup sugar
1 (8 oz.) topping, thawed
1 (20 oz.) can cherry pie filling

Instructions

Cream cheese with sugar; add milk and mix well. Combine with the thawed topping. Remove the brown crumbs from the cake. Break or cut cake into small pieces. Mix cake with the creamed mixture. Pour into a 9" x 13" pan. Combine pie filling and the flavoring. Place cherries on top. Can serve from a glass bowl. Keeps well for several days in refrigerator.

Menu: Ham and Red Pepper Quiche

SAINT PATRICK'S DAY

Tuna Salad with Green Peppercorn Dressing

Tuna Salad with Green Peppercorn Dressing

Fruity Pasta Salad

Broccoli Slaw

St. Patrick's Day Cake

I like the passion of a Saint Patrick's Day celebration and I am sure that I would like Ireland. I worked with several men from there who kept me entertained with dry humor emanating from Gaelic-influenced English. If I wrote a song about Ireland it would have to contain a lyric similar to a line in James Taylor's *"Mexico," "I've never been there but I'd sure like to go."*

- Bill

SAINT PATRICK'S DAY

Tuna Salad with Green Peppercorn Dressing

Ingredients

2 Tbs. chopped red onion
3 eggs boiled and chopped
½ cup minced red bell pepper
2 Tbs. green peppercorns
1 Tbs. sherry, optional
2 Tbs. fresh squeezed
lemon juice
3 Tbs. mayonnaise
1 Tbs. whole grain mustard
6 ½ oz. white chunk
tuna packed in water, drained
Seasonal greens

Instructions

1. Toss together the red onion, eggs, red peppers, green peppercorns, sherry, lemon juice, mayonnaise, and mustard.

2. Gently, stir in the tuna. Season to taste with salt and pepper. Chill for at least 2 hours or until serving time. Serve chilled on a bed of greens.

I put the boiled eggs on the side rather than include them in the salad.

Menu: Tuna Salad with Green Peppercorn Dressing

SAINT PATRICK'S DAY

Fruity Pasta Salad

Ingredients

1 1 lb. package campanelle (bell flower) pasta or bow-tie pasta
8 oz. fresh sugar snap or snow pea pods, trimmed (2 ½ cups)
3 cups cubed honeydew melon
1 cup purchased poppy-seed dressing
1 ½ tsp. finely shredded orange peel
4 cups strawberries, hulled and quartered lengthwise
1 ½ cups honey-roasted cashews (optional)
Additional purchased poppy-seed dressing (optional)

Instructions

1. In a Dutch oven or large pot cook pasta in salted boiling water according to package directions, adding the pea pods to the pasta the last 1 minute of cooking. Drain pasta and pea pods. Rinse with cold water and drain again. Transfer to a very large mixing bowl. Add melon and toss to combine.

2. In a small bowl stir together the dressing and orange peel. Add to pasta mixture and toss to coat. Cover and chill up to 24 hours.

3. To serve, gently stir in the strawberries and, if desired, nuts. If necessary, stir in up to ½ cup additional poppy-seed dressing to moisten. Transfer to a serving bowl. Makes 25 servings.

Menu: Tuna Salad with Green Peppercorn Dressing

SAINT PATRICK'S DAY

Broccoli Slaw

Ingredients

1 (12 oz.) package fresh broccoli slaw
1 cup red seedless grapes, halved
1 Granny Smith apple, diced
1 cup Vidalia onion or poppy seed dressing
2 oranges, peeled and sectioned, or canned mandarin oranges
Toasted chopped pecans (optional)

Instructions

Stir together first 5 ingredients in a large bowl. Top with chopped pecans, if desired.

Menu: Tuna Salad with Green Peppercorn Dressing

St. Patrick's Day Cake

Ingredients

Angel food cake (store bought or made from mix)
1 ½ cups cold milk
1 envelope Cream Whip Topping Mix
1 pkg. (4 serving size) Pistachio Flavor Jell-O Instant Pudding

Instructions

Prepare cake for frosting by wiping with moist cloth to remove brownish crumbs.
Prepare frosting as follows:
Pour cold milk into deep bowl; add Dream Whip and Instant pudding mix. Beat slowly to blend. Gradually increase to high speed until mixture forms soft peaks. Frost cake immediately. Decorate as desired.

Menu: Tuna Salad with Green Peppercorn Dressing

GARDEN LUNCHEON

Garden Luncheon Menu

BBQ Shrimp & Grits

Barbecue Shrimp

Garlic-Cheese Grits

Asparagus with Dill Sauce

Ranch Biscuits with Ham

Spiked Strawberries

Many people from outside of the southeast are not familiar with grits. This menu is the icebreaker for those who are skeptical. Shrimp 'N Grits is a coastal delicacy enjoyed in the states bordering the Gulf of Mexico and Atlantic Ocean up to the Carolinas, (maybe into Virginia).

Worthy of note is that the quality of the grits excels when using stone-ground rather than "instant." Stone-ground grits might be rare in the regular grocery store if you are not in the southeast U.S. We normally pick up a supply at the Asheville, NC Farmers' Market when we are in that area.

(Also, they can be ordered on-line.)

– Lynn

GARDEN LUNCHEON

Barbecue Shrimp

Ingredients

6 ¼ lb. unpeeled, medium-size fresh shrimp
½ cup butter, melted
¼ cup Worcestershire sauce
¼ cup lemon juice
1 Tbs. Old Bay seasoning
1 Tbs. coarsely ground pepper
1 to 2 garlic cloves, minced
1 Tbs. Cajun seasoning
1 Tbs. hot sauce

Instructions

Peel shrimp, and devein, if desired. Combine shrimp and remaining ingredients in a lightly greased large shallow roasting pan; toss to coat. Arrange shrimp in a single layer. Bake at 350°F. for 15 to 20 minutes or until shrimp turn pink, stirring occasionally. Yield: 25 servings.

Peel shrimp a day ahead, and store in zip-top plastic bags in refrigerator.

Garlic-Cheese Grits

Ingredients

3-½ qt. water
1 ½ Tbs. salt
4 cups uncooked stone-ground grits
5 garlic cloves, minced
1 (2 lb.) loaf process cheese spread, cubed
1 cup half-and-half
⅔ cup butter or margarine

Instructions

Bring water and salt to a boil in a large Dutch oven; gradually stir in grits and garlic. Cover; reduce heat, and simmer, stirring occasionally, 10 minutes.Add cheese, half-and-half, and butter; simmer, stirring constantly, until cheese and butter melt. Yield: 36 servings.

These may be made about 1 hour before the event; they reheat perfectly over low heat.

Menu: BBQ Shrimp & Grits

GARDEN LUNCHEON

Asparagus with Dill Sauce

Ingredients

1 cup mayonnaise
1 (8 oz.) container sour cream
1 Tbs. minced onion
1 tsp. dried dill weed
3 Tbs. lemon juice
2 lb. asparagus
2 Tbs. lemon juice

Instructions

Combine first 5 ingredients; cover and chill.Snap tough ends from asparagus. Arrange asparagus in a steamer basket over boiling water; cover and steam 4 to 5 minutes or until crisp-tender. Arrange asparagus on a serving platter; drizzle with 2 Tbs. lemon juice. Serve with sauce. Yield: 25 servings.

Steam asparagus up to 2 days ahead and store in zip-top plastic bags in refrigerator. Make dill sauce up to 3 days ahead; refrigerate in an airtight container.

Ranch Biscuits with Ham

Ingredients

1 (¼ oz.) envelope active dry yeast
½ cup warm water (105° to 115°)
2 cups buttermilk
5-½ cups all-purpose flour
¼ cup sugar
1 ½ Tbs. baking powder
1 ½ tsp. salt
½ tsp. baking soda
¾ cup shortening
½ lb. shaved country ham

Instructions

Combine yeast and ½ cup warm water in a 4 cups liquid measuring cups; let mixture stand 5 minutes. Stir in buttermilk. Combine flour and nxt 4 ingredients in a large bowl; cut shortning into flour mixture until crumbley. Add buttermilk mixture, stirring with a fork just until dry ingredients are moist. Turn dough ontoa well floured surface and knead 4 or 5 times. Roll dough to ½ inch thickness; cut with 2" biscuit cutter and place on lightly greased baking sheets. Cover and let rise in a warm place (85°F.), free of drafts, 1 hour. Bake at 425°F. For 10-12 minutes or until lightly brown. Yield: 3 dozen.

Buy country ham and shave slices to tuck inside these light, tender biscuits. Make and freeze the biscuits up to 2 weeks ahead. Thaw and heat before assembling and serving.

Menu: BBQ Shrimp & Grits

GARDEN LUNCHEON

Spiked Strawberries

Ingredients

3 cups orange juice
1 ½ cups tequila
½ cup balsamic vinegar
6 qt. strawberries
Garnish: fresh mint sprigs

Instructions

Combine orange juice, tequila, and vinegar; pour over strawberries, and let stand 10 minutes. Drain. Garnish, if desired. Yield: 25 servings.

Make this at the last minute. The berries need only 10 minutes to drink in the flavor.

Menu: BBQ Shrimp & Grits

EASTER

Easter Menu

In the Vegetable Garden

Vegetable Garden with Yogurt Dill Dip

Marinated Chicken with Vegetables

Chocolate Walnut Pie

Hot Rolls (of your choice)

The **Vegetable Garden** *can be presented as a table-top garden surrounded by a white picket fence. See the book cover - front center photo.*

Make sure that you leave room for the chocolate walnut pie.

Ready to celebrate Easter

EASTER

What does the Easter Bunny, eggs and the moon have to do with Easter? Why does Easter always fall on Sunday? For that matter, what does the name "Easter," have to do with Easter?

The answer is nothing. We in the United States can blame it on the Pennsylvania Dutch in the 1700's, who, in turn, can point to the German Roman Catholics of the 15th Century who, in their tradition of keeping local traditions, merged the celebration of the resurrection of Christ with the Spring festival of Ostara, a Teutonic fertility goddess of pre-Christian 13th Century Germany whose English name is Eostra, updated to modern day English is "Easter."

So Ostara/Eostra/Easter not only names the Christians' sacred holiday, but also drags her baggage behind her and drops it on our modern day celebration – that is, her fertility symbol, the rabbit. Eggs now symbolize the Resurrection, but not until the 15th Century. Eggs are an ancient symbol of fertility and were pulled in with the rabbit.

Girls play in warm spring sun

In summary, by the 1500's, we had an Easter Bunny and in the 1600's, we heard stories about the bunny laying eggs and hiding them in the garden. In the 2000's, has the Easter Bunny become a substitute for the Christian celebration?
(Well, after all, the pagans got there first.)

What does the moon have to do with it?

In the year 325, the First Council of Nicaea defined the date of Easter as the first Sunday after the first full moon following the March equinox. Therefore, Easter always falls on Sunday!

EASTER

Vegetable Garden with Yogurt Dill Dip

Ingredients

Instructions

1 cup plain yogurt
(can use non-fat)
1 cup mayonnaise
½ tsp. garlic powder
½ tsp. onion powder
½ tsp. fresh lemon juice
2 Tbs. chopped
fresh dill

Combine the ingredients in a medium-size bowl and mix until smooth. Chill for several hours or overnight before serving.

Marinated Chicken with Vegetables

Ingredients

Instructions

¾ cup lite soy sauce
⅔ cup honey
⅓ cup dry sherry (⅓ cup
pineapple juice was
substituted for sherry)
½ tsp. Garlic powder
¼ tsp. Ground ginger
1 ½ lbs. fresh asparagus
spears
6 skinned and boned chicken
breast halves, ¾-inch strips
¼ cup stone-ground mustard
2 Tbs. sesame seeds, toasted
3 tomatoes, cut into wedges
8 cups mixed salad greens
Honey-Mustard Dressing

HONEY-MUSTARD DRESSING
1 (8 oz.) container light sour
cream
¼ cup reduced-fat mayonnaise
½ cup honey
2 Tbs. Stone-ground mustard
2 Tbs. Dijon mustard
2 Tbs. Lemon juice

STIR together first 5 ingredients; set ½ cup mixture aside. POUR remaining soy sauce mixture evenly into 2 heavy-duty zip-top plastic bags. Snap off tough ends of asparagus, and place asparagus spears in 1 bag. Add chicken to remaining bag. Seal and chill at least 2 hours.DRAIN chicken and asparagus, discarding marinade. Place chicken on a lightly greased roasting pan. Place chicken on a lightly greased roasting pan. Place asparagus in a lightly greased 13- x 9-inch pan. STIR together reserved ½ cup soy sauce mixture, mustard, and sesame seeds. Pour ½ cup mixture over chicken and remaining ¼ cup over asparagus. BAKE chicken at 425 for 5 minutes. Place asparagus in oven, and bake chicken and asparagus 10 minutes or until chicken is done. Cool, if desired. Place separately in zip-top plastic bags, and chill 8 hours, if desired. ARRANGE chicken, asparagus, and tomato over salad greens, and drizzle with Honey-Mustard Dressing. Yield: 6 servings.Prep: 25 min., Chill: 2 hrs., Bake: 15 min.

Menu: In the Vegetable Garden

EASTER

Chocolate Walnut Pie

Ingredients

3 large eggs
1½ cups sugar
6 Tbs. unsalted butter
2 tsp. vanilla
¾ cup all-purpose flour
1½ cups semi-sweet chocolate chips
1½ cups chopped walnuts
Pie crust
Vanilla ice cream
Chocolate shavings
Crème de cocco

Instructions

Make pate brisée (pie crust), your favorite recipe or buy ready made; roll the dough into a round ⅛-inch thick on a floured surface and fit it into a 9-inch pie plate. Trim the excess dough, crimp the edge decoratively, and chill the shell for 30 minutes.In a bowl combine 3 large eggs, beaten lightly, 1 ½ cups sugar, ¾ stick (6 Tbs.) unsalted butter, melted and cooled, and 2 tsp. vanilla and beat the mixture lightly until it is blended. Stir in ¾ cup all-purpose flour, add 1 ½ cups each of semi-sweet chocolate chips and chopped walnuts, and stir the mixture until it is well combined. Pour the filling into the shell and bake the pie in the lower third of a preheated moderate oven (350°F.) for 1 hour to 1 hour and 5 minutes, or until a cake tester inserted in the center comes out almost clean. Let the pie cool in the plate on a rack and chill it for at least 4 hours or overnight. Heat the pie in a preheated moderately hot oven (375°F.) for 10 minutes, or until it is just heated through, and serve it with vanilla ice cream topped with chocolate shavings and drizzled with crème de cacao.

A family favorite!

Menu: In the Vegetable Garden

SOUTH OF THE BORDER

Can you believe that the Cinco de Mayo *(May 5) is a bigger deal in the United States than it is in Mexico? In both countries the traditions include street festivals, parties and Mariachi music.*

This excuse for a party started when Napoleon decided to carve out a piece of Mexico for himself in payment for Mexico's debt to France in 1861. Mexico was in financial ruin but had negotiated its obligations to England and Spain.

Although the Mexican's struggled with French troops for six years thereafter, the well provisioned French army suffered a loss to the fortified Mexicans at Puebla de Los Angeles –just call it Puebla - on, (save the date), May 5, 1862.

That's a good enough reason for me to party – let's have some fun! We have two great menus to save the stomach from an all-out Margarita blitz.

– Bill

19th Century Soldier

Arroz con Pollo Menu

Arroz con Pollo

Fiesta Punch

Arroz con Pollo

South of the Border Salad

Mexican Corn Bread

Apple Enchiladas

Tres Leches Cake (Alternative dessert)

SOUTH OF THE BORDER

Note: Turn this punch

Fiesta Punch

Ingredients

Instructions

2 cups cranberry juice, chilled
1 (6 oz.) can frozen orange juice
concentrate (prepared according
to package directions), or 1 qt.
store-bought orange juice
2 Tbs. lemon juice
1 qt. raspberry or
strawberry soda, chilled
1 medium navel orange, sliced
1 lemon, sliced
1 lime, sliced

In a 2 ½ to 3 qt. pitcher, combine cranberry, orange and lemon juices. At serving time, add chilled soda and orange, lemon and lime slices.Serving suggestion: Garnish each glass with fruit kabobs (pineapple chunks, maraschino cherries, lemon, lime or orange wedges), if desired. Makes 2 ½ qt.

Turn it up a notch with Tequila, according to your taste.

Did you know that tequila was one of the first distilled spirits indigenous to North America? *(Thanks to the Spanish in the 1500's who settled around what would be the town of Tequila, established in the mid 1600's.)*

Whatever grows in the region somehow finds its way into a bottle of adult beverage. The agave plant turned out to be an excellent specimen resulting in tequila. Similar to grapes that turn into wine, the growing location and conditions affect the plants' characteristics such as sweetness, fragrance and flavor yielding different qualities in the tequila beverages.

Tequila can be either mixed with at least 51% agave or 100% agave. Different types reflect aging:
- *Raposado – aged up to one year*
- *Añejo – aged from one to three years*

What about the worm?
I'm not going there.

–Bill

SOUTH OF THE BORDER

Arroz con Pollo

Ingredients

8 cups chicken broth (Can make own or purchase. Be sure to watch for sodium content if you purchase.)

2 chickens, cut into 8 pieces, or 8 chicken quarters

2 cups sour orange juice or a mixture of equal parts orange and lemon juice

½ lb. ham cut in ½-inch cubes, optional

½ cup of extra-virgin olive oil

2 large onions, diced

2 green peppers, seeded and diced

2 red peppers, seeded and diced

2-3 cloves garlic, minced

6 plum tomatoes, peeled, seeded and diced or an 8 oz. can tomato sauce

2 envelopes Sazon Goya with saffron*

8 or 10 saffron threads, toasted and pulverized (optional, very expensive)

4 cups short grain rice (Valencia style) rinsed and drained

4 tsp. salt (or to taste)

½ tsp. freshly ground pepper

2 bay leaves

2 Tbs. minced fresh cilantro

1 cup good dry white wine (can use chicken stock)

1 (15 oz.) can tender green peas or 1 cup frozen peas

Instructions

1.   Toast the saffron in a small dry skillet for a few minutes over medium heat. Pulverize the saffron in a mortar or between 2 sheets of wax paper with the back of a wooden spoon.

2.   Marinate the chicken pieces in the sour orange juice or lemon and orange mixture at least for 2 hours, but preferably overnight.

3.   Place all the ingredients for the broth in a large pot, bring to a boil, reduce the heat and simmer for 1 hour. Strain and set aside.

4.   Cook the arroz con pollo in an extra large Dutch oven.

5.   Dry the chicken pieces with paper towels. Heat the oil in the pan over medium heat and in it sauté the chicken pieces. Add the ham and sauté also. Remove the chicken and ham from the pan and set aside. The chicken skin can be removed if you are concerned with fat.

6.   In the remaining oil in the pan, sauté the onion, sweet peppers and garlic for 4 to 5 minutes. Add the garlic last to prevent it from burning which will give the dish a bitter taste. Add the tomato and cook for 5 minutes longer over low heat.

7.   Add 2 Tbs. of Goya seasoning, the saffron, salt, cilantro and the bay leaves. Add the chicken and the ham and 8 cups of broth.

8.   Bring all to a boil, add the rice, and bring to a boil again. Stir, reduce the heat, cover, and simmer for 25 minutes.

9.   Remove the bay leaves, pour the wine (or broth) over all and gently fold in the peas.

*Sazon Goya with saffron is a seasoning mix found in Latin American markets or in the ethnic section of many supermarkets.

Menu: Arroz con Pollo

SOUTH OF THE BORDER

Garnish for Arroz con Pollo

Ingredients

1 (6 ½ oz.) can whole red
pimentos, sliced in strips
2 jars white (or green)
asparagus
1 can artichokes, halves
2 Tbs. chopped parsley

Instructions

1. All the garnishing ingredients are traditional and are placed in spokes radiating from the center, which is decorated with a small bunch of parsley.
2. Cover and let stand for about 5 minutes before serving.

Menu: Arroz con Pollo

South of the Border Salad

Ingredients

SALAD:
3 large ripe Haas avocados,
peeled and thinly sliced
Freshly squeezed lime juice
1 large head curly leaf lettuce
1 head radicchio
4 seedless oranges, peeled and
sliced thinly
1 jicama, peeled and shredded
1 cup halved seedless green
grapes
1 cup halved seedless red grapes
DRESSING:
1 very ripe Haas avocado
⅓ cup freshly squeezed orange
juice
¼ cup fresh lime juice
2 Tbs. honey
Salt and pepper to taste
Crushed red pepper flakes to
taste

Instructions

Squeeze lime juice onto each slice of avocado and make sure the entire surface is covered. In a large flat bowl or individual salad dishes, place a ring of green lettuce leaves around the outside. In the center, place a ring of radicchio leaves. Arrange the avocado and orange slices on the green lettuce. Place the jicama on the radicchio. Sprinkle the grapes over the top. In a blender puree all of the dressing ingredients until smooth. Drizzle over the salad.

Prepare the fruits and vegetables and store them separately (coat the avocado in the lime juice before storing) and mix together right before serving.

Menu: Arroz con Pollo

SOUTH OF THE BORDER

Mexican Cornbread

Ingredients

1 can green chilies
1 cup corn meal
¾ cup buttermilk
1 small can cream corn
½ tsp. soda
2 eggs
1 cup shredded
cheddar cheese

Instructions

Mix all together. Bake 40 minutes at 400°F. in desired pan, (prefer cast iron skillet).

Note: This recipe was given to me by my sister-in-law, Mary Hemphill. It's a family favorite.

Apple Enchiladas

Ingredients

1 (21 oz.) can apple pie filling
6 (8-inch) flour tortillas
1 tsp. ground cinnamon
½ cup butter
½ cup white sugar
½ cup brown sugar
½ cup water

Instructions

Preheat oven to 350°F. Grease a 2 qt. baking dish.Spoon about one heaping quarter cups of pie filling evenly down the center of each tortilla. Sprinkle with cinnamon; roll up, tucking edges; and place seam side down in prepared dish In a medium saucepan over medium heat, combine butter, white sugar, brown sugar and water. Bring to a boil, stirring constantly; reduce heat and simmer 3 minutes. Pour sauce over enchiladas and let stand 30 minutes. Bake in preheated oven 20 minutes, or until golden.

Note: If you want to reduce the sugar in this recipe, use peeled and sliced apples. I use tart apples like Granny Smith.

Menu: Arroz con Pollo

SOUTH OF THE BORDER

Alternative Dessert

Tres Leches Cake

Ingredients

CAKE:
1 Tbs. all-purpose flour
1 tsp. salt
4 large egg whites
⅔ cup sugar
1 tsp. Vanilla
1 Tbs. lime zest
3 large eggs
⅔ cup all-purpose flour
MILK MIXTURE:
1 cup half and half (use light version)
1 (14 oz.) fat free sweetened condensed milk
1 (12 oz.) can fat free evaporated milk

Instructions

Preheat oven to 350°F. To prepare cake, coat a 13 x 9 inch baking dish with cooking spray; dust with 1 Tbs. flour. Place salt and 4 egg whites in a large bowl; beat with a mixer at high speed until soft peaks form. Gradually add ⅔ cup sugar, 1 Tbs. at a time, beating until soft peaks form. Place 1 tsp. vanilla and eggs in a large bowl; beat until thick and pale (about 3 minutes). Gently fold egg white mixture into egg mixture. Lightly spoon ⅔ cup flour into dry measuring cups; level with a knife. Gently put flour into egg mixture. Spoon batter into prepared dish. Bake at 350°F. for 20 minutes or until cake springs back when touched lightly in center. Cool 5 minutes in pan on a wire rack. To prepare the milk mixture, combine the half and half, condensed milk, and evaporated milk. Pour over the cake. Refrigerate cake for at least 2 hours before frosting. Serve with fresh fruit and a dollop of whipped cream

Menu: Arroz con Pollo

SOUTH OF THE BORDER

Pollo a La Parrilla Menu

Pollo a la Parrilla

Grilled Chicken with Black Bean and Mango-Pineapple Salsa

Tijuana-Caesar Salad

Saffron Rice

Fiesta Pumpkin Corn Muffins

Margarita Strawberry Dessert

SOUTH OF THE BORDER

Grilled Chicken with Black Bean and Mango-Pineapple Salsa

Ingredients

4 boneless, skinless chicken breasts (about 1 ½-2 lb. total)
¼ cup plus 2 Tbs. olive oil
¼ cup white wine vinegar
1 ½ Tbs. coarsely grated ginger
1 ½ Tbs. Dijon mustard
1 ½ tsp. ground coriander
1 ½ tsp. ground cumin
Freshly ground black pepper
2 ripe mangoes, peeled, pitted, and cut into ½-inch pieces
1 can (15 oz.) black beans, rinsed and drained
1 cup chopped fresh pineapple, in ½-inch pieces
½ cup finely diced red onion
¼ cup chopped fresh cilantro, plus optional sprigs for garnish
3 Tbs. freshly squeezed lime juice
2 tsp. minced garlic
½ jalapeno chile, cored, seeded, and minced
Dried red pepper flakes
Salt

Instructions

For the marinade, whisk together the oil, vinegar, ginger, mustard, coriander, and cumin in a small bowl and add pepper to taste. Put the chicken in a large resealable plastic bag and pour all but 2 Tbs. of the marinade over the chicken. Securely seal the bag and turn to evenly coat the chicken in the marinade. Refrigerate 1 to 2 hours, turning the bag occasionally. Set aside the reserved marinade for basting the chicken on the grill.

Mango-Pineapple Salsa: Combine the mangoes, black beans, pineapple, onion, cilantro, lime juice, garlic, and jalapeno with red pepper flakes to taste. Mix gently but thoroughly, season to taste with salt, cover with plastic, and refrigerate until ready to serve.

To grill: Preheat an outdoor grill (to high, if using a gas grill) and oil the grill grate. Take the chicken from the marinade, allowing excess to drip off, and grill it over medium-high heat, basting each side with the reserved marinade, turning only once. Grill until the chicken is cooked through (juice run clear when pierced with the tip of a knife in the thickest part), 10 to 12 minutes total. Take the chicken from the grill and cut each breast diagonally into ½-inch strips. To serve, spread the salsa on a serving platter or individual plates and arrange each breast on top in a fan shape. Garnish with sprigs of cilantro.
Makes 4 servings. Salsa also great served with broiled halibut or swordfish.

Menu: Pollo a la Parrilla

SOUTH OF THE BORDER

Tijuana-Caesar Salad

Ingredients

Cooking spray
3 flour tortillas (6 to 8 inches in diameter0
½ tsp. garlic salt
½ tsp. cumin
⅓ cup Caesar dressing
2 Tbs. grated lemon peel
1 Tbs. juice
6 cups bite-size pieces romaine (6 oz.)
4 oz. jicama, cut into cubes (1 cup)
1 medium red bell pepper, cut into thin strips (1 cup)
¼ cup shredded Parmesan cheese

Instructions

Heat oven to 375°F. Spray cookie sheet with cooking spray. Spray tortillas lightly with cooking spray. Sprinkle with garlic salt and cumin. Cut each tortilla in half, then crosswise into ½-inch strips. Place on cookie sheet. Bake 7 to 9 minutes or until crisp. Mix dressing, lemon peel and lemon juice. Toss romaine, jicama, bell pepper, tortilla strips, cheese and dressing mixture in large bowl. Sprinkle with additional shredded Parmesan cheese if desired. Serve immediately.

Note: For an authentic variation, ½ lb. cooked small shrimp can be added to this salad.

Menu: Pollo a la Parrilla

Saffron Rice

Ingredients

⅓ cup pine nuts
2 Tbs. butter or margarine
½ cup chopped onion, finely chopped
2 medium cloves garlic, minced
1 tsp. saffron threads or ¼ tsp. powdered saffron
1 cup rice, uncooked
2 cups chicken stock
2 Tbs. fresh parsley, finely chopped

Instructions

Toast pine nuts by sautéing them in a small, dry skillet over medium heat about 2 minutes or until they are golden. Set aside. Melt butter in a medium saucepan over medium heat. Add onion and cook until soft but not brown, about 5 minutes. Add garlic and saffron, cook 2 minutes longer. Add rice and stir to coat. Add chicken stock, bring to a boil, cover, reduce heat and simmer 17 to 20 minutes, until rice is tender. Stir in parsley and pine nuts. Serve immediately. Serves 4.

Menu: Pollo a la Parrilla

SOUTH OF THE BORDER

Fiesta Pumpkin Corn Muffins

Ingredients

1 cup yellow cornmeal
1 cup whole wheat flour (or white flour)
½ tsp. chili powder
2 Tbs. sugar (can omit)
4 tsp. baking powder
½ tsp. salt
2 eggs
1 cup cooked mashed pumpkin or canned pumpkin
1 cup milk
2 Tbs. vegetable oil
1 4 oz. can chopped green chilies
1 cup shredded cheddar cheese

Instructions

Preheat oven to 400 °F. In a large bowl mix the dry ingredients. In a smaller bowl, beat the eggs. Blend I the pumpkin, milk, and oil. Fold in the chilies. Blend the wet ingredients into the dry until the batter is just barely moistened. Spoon into greased or papered muffin cups. Sprinkle with the cheese and bake for 20-25 minutes or until a toothpick inserted in the middle comes out clean. Remove from the pan immediately and serve warm. Can be baked ahead and reheated before serving.Makes 12 muffins.

Margarita Strawberry Dessert

Ingredients

1 ½ cups crushed pretzels
¼ cup sugar
½ cup margarine, melted
1 (14 oz.) can sweetened condensed milk
½ cup frozen margarita mix concentrate, thawed
1 (10 oz.) package frozen strawberries in syrup, thawed
8 oz. whipped topping, or 2 cups heavy whipping cream, whipped

Instructions

Mix the pretzels, sugar and melted margarine in a bowl. Press firmly onto the bottom of an ungreased 8- or 9-inch springform pan; chill.Combine the sweetened condensed milk and margarita mix in a large bowl. Beat with an electric mixer until smooth. Add the strawberries and beat at low speed until mixed. Fold in the whipped topping. Pour into the prepared crust. Cover and freeze for at least 3 hours or overnight. Let stand at room temperature for 30 minutes before serving. Serves 10.

Menu: Pollo a la Parrilla

PACIFIC RIM

Worry not! This Pacific Rim does not contain aliens or giant robots as displayed in the 2013 Film by Guillermo del Toro.

– Bill

Noodle-Chicken Menu

Soba Noodle/Mahogany Chicken Salad

Soba Noodle Salad with Passion Fruit Vinaigrette

Mahogany Chicken

Congealed Mandarin Orange Salad

Angel Biscuits

Coconut-Guava Thumb-Print Cookies

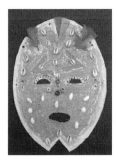

"Mask," Black & white copy of color original by Ruby Wolter

The operative item in this menu is "Mahogany Chicken." Beware of other recipes for mahogany chicken. Lynn's recipe calls for hoisin sauce and Chinese plum sauce. Not that the others are less notable, but if you want to get the same result that happens in our house where everyone salivates in excitement over the Mahogany Chicken, use Lynn's recipe.

– Bill

PACIFIC RIM

Soba Noodle Salad with Passion Fruit Vinaigrette

Ingredients

½ lb. soba noodles (see note)
1 tsp. Asian sesame oil
½ lb. mixed baby salad greens
¼ cup julienned
red bell peppers
¼ cup peeled and julienned
carrots
¼ cup julienned snow peas
2 Tbs. sliced pickled ginger
(can use fresh or omit)
1 Tbs. sesame seeds, toasted
2 Tbs. chopped green onions,
green part only
2 Tbs. chopped fresh cilantro
2 Tbs. chopped fresh mint,
plus 1 sprig for garnish

Instructions

Bring a large pot of salted water to a boil. Add the soba noodles, stir well, and cook for 6 to 7 minutes, until al dente. Drain and rinse with cool water. Cut the noodles with scissors to achieve shorter lengths. Place in a bowl, add the sesame oil, and toss well. In a separate bowl, toss the greens with the vinaigrette. In a large, nice glass bowl, arrange a layer of one-third of the greens. Top with a layer of one-third of the noodles. Sprinkle the noodles with one-third each of the bell pepper, carrot, snow peas, ginger, sesame seeds, green onion, cilantro, and mint. Repeat to make 2 additional layers of greens, noodles, vegetables, and seasonings. Garnish with the sprig of mint and serve with salad tongs to include all the layers in each serving.Makes 4 servings.

NOTE: If you can't find soba noodles, spaghetti will do. And if you can't find passion fruit, substitute concentrated frozen orange juice. I used Hawaii's Own Passion-Orange concentrated frozen juice.

Passion Fruit Vinaigrette

Ingredients

5 Tbs. passion fruit puree (see note)
1 clove garlic, minced
½ tsp. Dijon mustard
2 tsp. sugar
1 tsp. freshly squeezed lemon juice
¾ cup olive oil

Instructions

To prepare the vinaigrette, in a blender, combine all the ingredients and process until well blended. Set aside.

Menu: Soba Noodle/Mahogany Chicken Salad

PACIFIC RIM

Mahogany Chicken

Ingredients

1½ cups soy sauce
1⅛ cups Hoisin Sauce
¾ cup Chinese Plum Sauce
18 green onions, minced
6 large garlic cloves, minced
¾ cup cider vinegar
1 cup honey
6 to 7 lb. chicken

Note: I usually use drumettes.

Instructions

In 3 qt. saucepan, combine all ingredients except chicken. Bring to a boil and simmer 5 minutes. Cool. Pour cooled sauce over chicken; cover and refrigerate overnight. Place oven racks in upper and lower thirds of oven and preheat to 375°F. Line 2 large shallow roasting pans with foil that has been sprayed with oil. Drain chicken; reserve marinade to use throughout cooking for basting. Divide chicken between prepared pans and bake uncovered 45 minutes to 1 hour (time is approximate), basting about every 20 minutes with remaining sauce and turning to brown evenly. Be sure to switch the pans halfway through cooking. Remove chicken from pans and let cool on large sheets of foil. When cool, wrap and store for up to 3 days. With Soba Noodle Salad, slice and serve at room temperature. This has been a family favorite for over 30 years.

The Hali'imaile General Store Cookbook had become one of my favorites, so on our first trip to Maui, we drove up-country and found the store and restaurant located among lush pineapple fields. The food was delicious. If you have the opportunity and make the visit, you will not be disappointed. I was extremely pleased with the Soba Noodle and Passion Fruit Venaigrette from that cookbook as well as the Chinese Chicken Salad (on page 76).
- Lynn

Congealed Mandarin Orange Salad

Ingredients

1 3 oz. package orange Jell-O
1 cup hot tea (see note)
1 cup crushed pineapple, drained
1 (11 oz.) can mandarin oranges
1 cup reserved fruit juices
1 cup water chestnuts, chopped
Garnish: cream cheese, sprinkle of mace, orange slice

Instructions

Dissolve Jell-O in hot tea. Drain pineapple and oranges, reserving juices. Add pineapple, oranges, juices and water chestnuts to Jell-O. Pour mixture into a 4 cups salad mold and chill until set, approximately 3 hours. Garnish. Serves 8.

NOTE: Can use a flavored tea to add more zip, i.e., Celestial Seasonings Bengal Spice.

Menu: Soba Noodle/Mahogany Chicken Salad

PACIFIC RIM

Angel Biscuits

Ingredients

5 cups White Lily flour, sifted (plain)
1 tsp. baking soda
3 tsp. baking powder
1 tsp. salt
¼ cup sugar
1 cup Crisco
1 package yeast dissolved in 3 Tbs. warm water
2 cups buttermilk (room temperature)

Instructions

Sift flour with dry ingredients. Cut in shortening. Add yeast to buttermilk. Stir buttermilk mixture into flour mixture until all flour is damp. Refrigerate before using. * Do not roll out. Simply pinch off amount needed for each biscuit. Handle very lightly. Bake at 425°F. for 10 to 15 minutes or until brown. Yield: 4 dozen small biscuits.

*Dough can be kept a week covered tightly in the refrigerator.

Menu: Soba Noodle/Mahogany Chicken Salad

Coconut-Guava Thumbprint Cookies

Ingredients

1 cup (2 sticks) unsalted butter, room temperature
¾ cup sugar
1 3½ oz. can flaked coconut
½ tsp. almond extract
2 ½ cups all purpose flour
¼ tsp. salt
¼ tsp. freshly grated nutmeg
½ cup (about) guava paste

Instructions

Using electric mixer, beat butter and sugar until fluffy. Mix in coconut and almond extract. Add flour, salt and nutmeg and blend just until smooth. Refrigerate dough to firm, if necessary. Preheat oven to 350°F. Roll dough into 2 tsp.-size balls. Arrange on ungreased baking sheets, spacing 1 inch apart. Make small indentation in center of each cookie, using handle of wooded spoon. Fill each indentation with ¼ tsp. guava paste. Bake cookies until light brown around edges, about 15 minutes. Cool on racks. Store in airtight container. (Can be prepared 1 month ahead and frozen.) Makes about 4 dozen cookies.

Menu: Soba Noodle/Mahogany Chicken Salad.

SAVANNAH JAMBALAYA

Savannah Jambalaya Menu

Savannah Jambalaya

Savannah Jambalaya

Fresh Orange Slices

Spinach Salad with Tarragon Vinaigrette

Tarragon Vinaigrette

French Bread

Almond-Butter Cake

Let's go to Savannah, Georgia to enjoy this dish- or stay home and follow the recipe.

Jambalaya is enjoyed across the Southeast from Louisiana to the Atlantic. It is a spicy rice dish with any desired meat like sausage and seafood, (especially shrimp), and tomatoes, peppers and hot sauces to taste. But why should that be detailed here?

Just read the recipe. -Bill

Recipe Origin Savannah, Ga

SAVANNAH JAMBALAYA

Savannah Jambalaya

Ingredients

4 Tbs. olive oil, divided
1 to 1 ¼ lb. boneless, skinless chicken thighs*
½ lb. hot Italian sausage links*
2 Tbs. butter or margarine
¼ lb. country-smoked ham or prosciutto ham, cut into ¼-inch dice*
1 cup (28 oz.) tomatoes in juice, diced (reserve juice)
1 cup chicken broth
1 lb. medium peeled and deveined shrimp*
½ cup finely chopped green pepper
1 tsp. thyme
1 tsp. oregano
½ tsp. freshly ground pepper
¼ tsp. salt
Chopped fresh parsley, for garnish

Instructions

1. Heat 1 Tbs. oil in medium Dutch oven over medium-high heat. Add chicken and sausage; cook, stirring occasionally, 8 to 10 minutes until browned. Transfer to cutting board with slotted spoon; cool and cut into 1-incn pieces. Set aside.

2. While the sausage cools, remove all but 1 Tbs. drippings from Dutch oven; add butter and melt over medium heat. Add ham and cook until browned, 3 to 5 minutes. Stir in onions and rice; cook 3 minutes. Add tomatoes and juice, broth and reserved chicken and sausage. Bring to a boil, cover and reduce heat to low. Cook until rice is tender and liquid is absorbed, about 25 minutes.

3. Meanwhile, combine remaining 3 Tbs. oil, shrimp, green pepper, thyme, oregano, pepper and salt in medium bowl. Cover with plastic wrap and refrigerate.

4. When rice is almost tender, heat large nonstick skillet over medium-high heat. Add shrimp mixture and cook, stirring occasionally, 3 to 5 minutes until shrimp is cooked through. Spoon shrimp over rice mixture. Garnish with parsley, if desired. Makes 6 servings.

*Can use any or all of these meats/seafoods. Turkey sausage, crab, scallops, etc., can also be used. NOTE: You can spice the dish up by adding cayenne pepper, Tabasco, chili powder, garlic, Worcestershire sauce, etc.

JAMBALAYA is a "leftover" dish. The name means "clean up the kitchen."

Menu: Savannah Jambalaya

SAVANNAH JAMBALAYA

Spinach Salad with Tarragon Vinaigrette

Ingredients	Instructions
SALAD: 10 oz. fresh spinach leaves 8 slices bacon 3 hard-cooked eggs, chopped ½ lb. fresh mushrooms, sliced ⅓ thinly sliced purple onion ¼ cup sesame seeds, toasted	To prepare Tarragon Vinaigrette, whisk together vinaigrette ingredients. Refrigerate. Dressing is more flavorful if made several hours in advance. (May be made up to 2 days ahead.) Wash and stem spinach. Tear into bite-size pieces. Cook bacon; drain and crumble. To assemble salad, toss spinach, eggs, mushrooms, and onion rings with desired amount of dressing. Toss in bacon and sesame seeds. Serve immediately.

Menu: Savannah Jambalaya

Tarragon Vinaigrette

Ingredients	Instructions
TARRAGON VINAIGRETTE: ¾ cup vegetable oil ½ cup red wine vinegar 2 Tbs. sugar 1 clove garlic, crushed 1 tsp. Worcestershire sauce 2 drops Tabasco Sauce ½ tsp. salt ¼ tsp. freshly ground pepper ½ tsp. dried tarragon ½ tsp. dry mustard	Mix ingredients together. Nothing more – nothing less.

Menu: Savannah Jambalaya

SAVANNAH JAMBALAYA

Almond-Butter Cake

Ingredients

INGREDIENTS:
1 ½ cups sugar
1 cup packed (about 10 oz.)
almond paste, at room
temperature
1 ⅓ cups salted butter,
at room temperature
½ tsp. vanilla extract
1 ⅓ cups unsifted
all-purpose flour
1 tsp. baking powder

Instructions

Preheat oven to 350°F. Place sugar in the work bowl of a food processor equipped with a steel blade. Break almond paste into rough chunks and add to work bowl. Process until almond paste and sugar are thoroughly combined (a couple of minutes). Add butter 2 Tbs. or so at a time, processing until mixture is smooth, scraping sides of work bowl with a spatula several times. Then add eggs, one at a time, processing until each is incorporated. Add vanilla and process very briefly to combine. In a separate bowl, mix together flour and baking powder. Add to the batter in the food processor and process until well blended, being careful not to over-process. You will need to scrape the sides of the work bowl once or twice. Line two 8 or 9 inch cake pans with foil. Fill each liner two-thirds full with the batter (about ⅓ cup per liner—do not overfill), or distribute the batter evenly between the two cake pans. Bake in upper third of the preheated oven for 50-60 minutes. Test for doneness by touching the middle of a cake. If the cake is firm to the touch and springs back with no indentation, the cake is done. If not, bake a few minutes more and test again. When done, remove the cakes from the oven. Remove the layer cakes from their pans by lifting the foil. Place them on racks and let them cool in the foil. When cakes are cool, remove foil and frost, if desired.

This is a moist cake and will keep for several days. Ice as you like, (chocolate, boiled frosting, cream cheese, etc.) or serve plain with fresh friut and whipped cream.

Menu: Savannah Jambalaya

THE HOLIDAYS

Pork Tenderloin / Cranberry-Orange Relish Menu

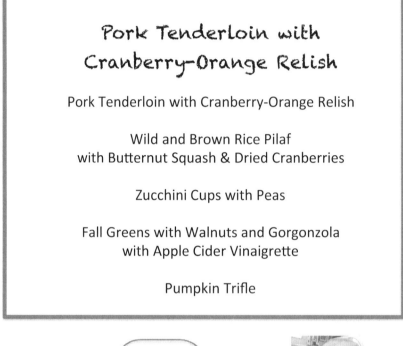

Pork Tenderloin with Cranberry-Orange Relish

Pork Tenderloin with Cranberry-Orange Relish

Wild and Brown Rice Pilaf
with Butternut Squash & Dried Cranberries

Zucchini Cups with Peas

Fall Greens with Walnuts and Gorgonzola
with Apple Cider Vinaigrette

Pumpkin Trifle

...I am thankful for...

Record of a conversation of one Native American to another:

"That togetherness feast with the Pilgrims was ok but I wouldn't want to make it an annual affair."

(Sorry, I guess it caught on.)   *- Bill*

THE HOLIDAYS

Pork Tenderloin with Cranberry-Orange Relish

Ingredients

1 (1 lb.) pork tenderloin
4 cups water
2 Tbs. sugar
1 Tbs. salt
1-½ tsp. dried thyme
1 tsp. whole allspice
1 bay leaf
1 tsp. dried rosemary, crushed
4 tsp. olive oil, divided
Cooking spray
¾ cup purchased cranberry–orange relish

Instructions

Trim fat from pork. Combine pork and next 6 ingredients in a large Ziploc plastic bag. Seal and marinate in refrigerate 2 ½ hours. Preheat oven to 350˚F. Remove pork from bags; discard marinade. Pat pork dry with a paper towel. Combine rosemary and 1 tsp. oil; rub over pork. Heat remaining 3 tsp. oil in a nonstick skillet over medium-high heat. Add pork; cook 5 minutes, browning on all sides. Place pork on broiler pan coated with cooking spray. Insert meat thermometer into thickest portion of pork. Bake at 350˚F. for 35 minutes or until thermometer registers 160˚F. (slightly pink). Serve with cranberry-orange relish.

Menu: Pork Tenderloin with Cranberry-Orange Relish

Cranberry-Orange Relish

Ingredients

4 cups fresh or frozen cranberries
2 seedless oranges
2 cups sugar

Instructions

Place the cranberries in the food processor and chop. Slice the oranges into chunks, but leave the peel on. Add to the processor and chop until fine. Mix the sugar into the mixture and chill for at least 24 hours.

Makes 10 servings.

From Cooking Light, December 1996

Menu: Pork Tenderloin with Cranberry-Orange Relish

THE HOLIDAYS

Wild and Brown Rice Pilaf
with Butternut Squash & Dried Cranberries

Ingredients

2 Tbs. olive oil
1 cup chopped onions
½ cup chopped peeled carrot
1 Tbs. minced peeled ginger
1 Tbs. curry powder
1 tsp. ground cumin
1 garlic clove, minced
3 cups (½-inch cubes) peeled seeded butternut squash
1 cup wild rice
1 cup long-grain brown rice
1 Fuji apple, peeled, cored, diced
1 cinnamon stick
3-¾ cups water
2 tsp. salt
½ cup dried cranberries

Instructions

Heat oil in heavy large saucepan over medium heat. Add onion and carrot; sauté 5 minutes. Add ginger, curry powder, cumin, and garlic; stir 1 minute. Stir in squash and next 4 ingredients. Add 3¾ cups water and salt. Bring to boil. Reduce heat to medium-low, cover, and simmer until water is absorbed and rice is tender, about 45 minutes. Remove from heat. Stir in cranberries. Cover, let stand until cranberries soften, about 10 minutes. Season to taste with salt and pepper. Transfer to bowl. (Can be made 2 hours ahead of time. Let stand uncovered at room temperature. Cover with plastic wrap; rewarm in microwave.)

Menu: Pork Tenderloin with Cranberry-Orange Relish

THE HOLIDAYS

Zucchini Cups with Peas

Ingredients

5 (1 lb.) 2 ½-inch diameter zucchini, ends trimmed
2 Tbs. (¼ stick) butter, melted
Salt
¼ cup butter
½ cup minced onion
2 garlic cloves, minced
2 ½ cups frozen tiny peas, thawed
½ tsp. dried tarragon, crumbled
½ tsp. salt
¼ tsp. freshly ground white pepper
1 tsp. fresh lemon juice
Lemon slices
Tarragon sprigs

Instructions

Peel lengthwise strips from zucchini to create striped appearance. Cut into 1 ½-inch lengths. Hollow out pieces from one end using melon baller, leaving ¼-inch-thick sides and ½-inch base. Reserve zucchini balls. Cook zucchini cups in large pot of boiling salted water until crisp-tender, about 4 minutes. Rinse with cold water and drain thoroughly. Brush all over with melted butter. Sprinkle inside with salt. Stand in baking dish. Melt ¼ cup butter in heavy medium saucepan over medium-low heat. Add onion and cook until soft, stirring frequently, about 8 minutes. Add zucchini balls and garlic and stir just until zucchini begins to soften, about 3 minutes. Add peas, dried tarragon, salt and pepper. Stir 1 minute. Add lemon juice. Spoon mixture into zucchini cups. (Can be prepared 1 day ahead and refrigerated. Bring zucchini to room temperature before continuing.) Preheat oven to 400°F. Bake zucchini until hot, about 7 minutes. Garnish with lemon slices and tarragon sprigs and serve immediately.

Menu: Pork Tenderloin with Cranberry-Orange Relish

Fall Greens with Walnuts and Gorgonzola

Ingredients

1 lb. mixed fall greens
1 apple (Braeburn, Red Delicious, or your own personal favorite)
½ cup walnuts, lightly toasted
⅓ cup crumbled Gorgonzola cheese
1 recipe Apple Cider Vinaigrette

Instructions

Place washed greens in a large salad bowl. Dice apple into ¼-inch pieces, leaving peel on. Toss walnuts, greens, apples, and Gorgonzola with vinaigrette immediately before serving.

Menu: Pork Tenderloin with Cranberry-Orange Relish

THE HOLIDAYS

Apple Cider Vinaigrette

Ingredients

1 cup apple cider
¼ cup apple cider
vinegar
2 tsp. brown sugar
1 tsp. Dijon mustard
⅛ tsp. kosher or sea salt
⅛ tsp. freshly ground
black pepper
⅔ cup vegetable oil

Instructions

Heat apple cider in a small saucepan and simmer over medium heat until reduced to approximately ¼ cup, about 15 minutes. Cool. Blend all vinaigrette ingredients together.

Menu: Pork Tenderloin with Cranberry-Orange Relish

Pumpkin Trifle

Ingredients

1 package (14 ½ oz.)
gingerbread cake mix
(Betty Crocker)
1 ¼ cups water
1 egg
4 cups cold fat-free milk
4 packages (1 oz.) sugar-free
instant butterscotch
pudding mix
1 can (15 oz.) solid-pack
pumpkin
1 tsp. cinnamon
¼ tsp. each ground ginger,
nutmeg and allspice
1 carton (12 oz.) reduced-fat
frozen whipped topping,
thawed

Instructions

In a mixing bowl, combine the cake mix, water and egg; mix well. Pour into an ungreased 8-inch square baking pan. Bake at 350°F. for 35-40 minutes or until a toothpick inserted near the center comes out clean. Cool for 10 minutes before removing form pan to a wire rack. When completely cooked, crumble the cake. Set aside ¼ cup crumbs for garnish. In a bowl, whisk milk and pudding mixes for 2 minutes or until slightly thickened. Let stand for 2 minutes or until soft set. Stir in pumpkin and spices; mix well. In a trifle bowl or 3 ½ qt. glass serving bowl, layer a fourth of the cake crumbs, half of the pumpkin mixture, a fourth of the cake crumbs and half of the whipped topping. Repeat layers. Garnish with reserved cake crumbs. Serve immediately or refrigerate. Yield: 18 servings. Diabetic Exchanges: 2 starches, 1 fat.

Menu: Pork Tenderloin with Cranberry-Orange Relish

THE HOLIDAYS

Smoked Turkey Green Bean Bundles Menu

Smoked Turkey Green Bean Bundles

Smoked Turkey Green Bean Bundles with Dijon Dipping Sauce

Frozen Cranberry Salad

Mixed Grain Salad with Dried Fruit

Apple-Almond Cheesecake

Great Harvest Bread

Black & white copy of color original by Ruby Wolter

THE HOLIDAYS

Smoked Turkey Green Bean Bundles with Dijon Dipping Sauce

Ingredients

½ lb. white smoked turkey
from the deli, sliced
1 lb. green beans
fresh green onions
½ red bell pepper,
cut into long strips

Dijon dipping sauce:
1 Tbs. Dijon mustard
¼ cup vinegar
1 Tbs. honey
½ tsp. salt
¼ tsp. black pepper
¼ cup olive oil
¼ cup vegetable oil

Instructions

Cook green beans in boiling water for 2 minutes. Drain and rinse in cold water immediately. Cut smoked turkey in 3 inch wide strips lengthwise across the slice. Take a bundle of green beans with a red bell pepper. Wrap a strip of turkey around it crosswise and tie together with a green onion.

TO MAKE DIPPING SAUCE: Blend mustard, vinegar, honey, salt and pepper together in a blender or food processor. Add oil in a thin stream and blend until sauce is thick.

Menu: Smoked Turkey Green Bean Bundles

Frozen Cranberry Salad

Ingredients

2 (3 oz.) pkgs. cream
2 tsp. mayonnaise
2 tsp. sugar
1 lb. can whole
cranberry sauce
1 (7 oz.) can crushed
pineapple, drained
½ cup chopped nuts
1 cup whipped cream

Instructions

Soften cheese. Blend in mayonnaise and sugar. Add fruits and nuts. Fold in whipped cream. Pour in loaf pan. Freeze firm. Cut in squares. Serves 8-10.

Menu: Smoked Turkey Green Bean Bundles

THE HOLIDAYS

Mixed Grain Salad with Dried Fruit

Ingredients

¼ cup vegetable oil
½ cup chopped shallots
1 cup brown rice
1 cup wild rice
1 cup wheat berries*
2 cups water
2 cups chicken
stock or canned
low-salt chicken broth
¾ cup dried cranberries
½ cup chopped
dried apricots
½ cup dried currants
½ cup Sherry wine vinegar
2 Tbs. walnut oil
or olive oil
2 Tbs. chopped fresh sage
or 2 tsp. dried rubbed sage
1 cup coarsely
chopped pecans

Instructions

Heat oil in large saucepan over medium-high heat. Add shallots and sauté until transluscent, about 5 minutes. Add brown rice, wild rice and wheat berries; stir to coat. Add 2 cups water and 2 cups stock. Bring to boil. Reduce heat to low Cover and cook until grains are tender and liquid is absorbed, about 40 minutes. Remove from heat. Stir cranberries, apricots and currants into grains. Cool to room temperature. Whisk vinegar, walnut oil and sage in small bowl to blend. Pour over salad and toss to coat. Season generously with salt and pepper. (Can be prepared 1 day ahead. Cover and refrigerate. Bring to room temperature before serving.) Stir pecans into salad and serve.

Menu: Smoked Turkey Green Bean Bundles

* (Also called hard wheat berries, available at natural foods stores)

THE HOLIDAYS

Apple-Almond Cheesecake

Ingredients

Instructions

CRUST:
1 cup graham cracker crumbs
1 cup sliced almonds, toasted
6 Tbs. (¾ stick) unsalted butter, melted
2 Tbs. golden brown sugar
¼ tsp. Salt

FILLING:
1 ½ 7 oz. packages almond paste, crumbled
3 8 oz. packages cream cheese, room temperature
6 Tbs. sugar
4 large eggs

APPLES:
4 large Jonagold apples (about 2 ½ lb.), peeled, cored, cut into ⅓-inch-thick slices
2 Tbs. fresh lemon juice
4 Tbs. unsalted butter
¾ cup (packed) golden brown sugar
¾ tsp. ground cinnamon

CRUST: Preheat oven to 350F. Butter 10-inch-diameter springform pan. Wrap bottom with 2 layers of heavy-duty foil. Mix all ingredients in medium bowl to blend, crumbling almonds slightly. Press mixture onto bottom and 1 inch up sides of pan. Bake until set, about 7 minutes. Maintain oven temperature.FILLING: Combine almond paste, cream cheese, and sugar in processor; blend until smooth, occasionally scraping down sides of bowl, about 2 minutes. Mix in eggs until just blended. Pour filling into crust. Bake 15 minutes. Reduce heat to 325F. and bake until center is set and top appears dry, about 45 minutes longer. Cool. Wrap in plastic and refrigerate overnight. (Can be prepared 2 days ahead. Keep refrigerated.)APPLES: Toss apple slices with lemon juice in large bowl. Melt 3 Tbs. butter in heavy large skillet over high heat. Add apples and sauté until golden and tender, stirring frequently, about 9 minutes. Sprinkle with brown sugar and cinnamon. Stir to cool. Add remaining 1 Tbs. butter. Stir until coated and glazed. Cool slightly.Run small sharp knife around edge of pan to loosen cheesecake. Release pan sides. Arrange apples (warm or room temperature) in concentric circles atop cheesecake. Brush apples with any juices left in skillet. Cut into wedges and serve.

12 Servings

Menu: Smoked Turkey Green Bean Bundles

THE HOLIDAYS

The Remains Of The Day Menu

Spicy Turkey Paella

Stuffing Stuffed Mushrooms

Marinated Vegetables with Garlic and Thyme

Spicy Turkey Paella

Cranberry-Citrus Sorbet

or Winter Fruit Plate

How many of us, after Thanksgiving, around Nov 27 – 28, for the third or fourth day of carving on an over-sized bird that barely looked eaten for the holiday meal, [but Mama says, "I ain't cooking again until it's all gone"], are sick and tired of gnawing on this left-over carcass?

Well it doesn't have to be! Lynn to the rescue - better than "Jim Dandy*," Lynn has the perfect solution.

I can stomach this spicy turkey paella for much longer than a dry turkey carcass. Give it a try some year after T-Day.
— Bill

* "Jim Dandy to the Rescue," recorded by LaVern Baker in 1956, one of Rolling Stone's 500 Greatest Songs

THE HOLIDAYS

Stuffing Stuffed Mushrooms

Ingredients

2 cups leftover stuffing
1 cup grated provolone cheese
(about 3 oz.)
1 large egg, lightly beaten
¼ cup chopped fresh parsley
¼ cup chopped fresh basil
¼ cup chopped green onions,
chopped
1 Tbs. olive oil (optional)
18 large button mushroom
(about 1 lb.), stems removed
Olive oil

Instructions

Preheat oven to 400°F. Break up stuffing into bowl. Add ¾ cup cheese, egg, parsley, basil, and green onions; mix well. If mixture seems dry, add 1 Tbs. olive oil to moisten. Season with salt and pepper. Scoop out center of mushroom caps using small spoon. Fill each mushroom with stuffing; place on rimmed baking sheet. Drizzle with olive oil and sprinkle with remaining ¼ cup cheese. Bake until stuffing is golden brown on top, about 15 minutes. Serve hot or at room temperature. Can be made 2 hours ahead. Let stand covered at room temperature. Serves 6

This menu is comprised of Thanksgiving leftovers in exotic disguises. Enjoy!

Marinated Vegetables with Garlic and Thyme

Ingredients

8 cups assorted cooked
leftover vegetables
(such as carrots, green
beans, cauliflower,
and broccoli)
2 cups grape tomatoes,
halved lengthwise
(about 1 lb.)
¾ cup olive oil
¼ cup red wine vinegar
2 Tbs. water
2 garlic cloves, pressed
1 tsp. dried thyme leaves
1 tsp. salt
½ tsp. sugar
½ tsp. hot pepper sauce

Instructions

Place cooked leftover vegetables in large strainer. Lower strainer into large pot of boiling water until butter and seasoning are removed, about 30 seconds. Rinse with cold water; pat dry. Transfer to large bowl and mix in tomatoes. Whisk all remaining ingredients in bowl; toss with vegetable mixture. Cover and refrigerate at least 6 hours and up to 2 days. Bring vegetables to room temperature. Season with salt and pepper; serve.Serves 6

Menu: The Remains of the Day

THE HOLIDAYS

Spicy Turkey Paella

Ingredients

12 oz. spicy smoked sausage cut into ½-inch slices
(such as linguica, andouille, hot links, or sausage of your choice)
¼ cup garlic-flavored olive oil
(Or add a clove of minced garlic when you stir in the rice)
2 large yellow onions, chopped
1 large red bell pepper, chopped
2 cups long-grain white rice
¼ tsp. saffron
4 cups low-salt chicken broth
4 large plum tomatoes, quartered
1 tsp. salt
1 tsp. dried oregano
½ tsp. cayenne pepper
4 ½ cup cooked leftover turkey, cut into ½-inch cubes
1 cup frozen peas

Instructions

Preheat oven to 350°F. Brown sausage in large skillet over medium-high heat, about 5 minutes. Remove from heat. Heat olive oil in 6½ qt. pot over medium-high heat. Add onions and cook until golden, stirring often, about 12 minutes.   Add bell pepper, cook 3 minutes, stirring frequently. Stir in rice and saffron, then next 5 ingredients. Bring to boil. Reduce heat to medium; cover and cook 15 minutes. Add sausage, turkey, and peas to rice mixture. Bake paella 10 minutes and serve. Serves 6.

Menu: The Remains of the Day

THE HOLIDAYS

Cheesecake Tart with Cranberry Glaze

Ingredients

CRUST:
1 ¾ cup graham
cracker crumbs
2 ½ Tbs. sugar
6 Tbs. (¾ stick) unsalted
butter, melted

FILLING:
3 cups chilled
whipping cream
2 tsp. unflavored gelatin
1 8 oz. package
cream cheese,
cut into pieces
1 cup chilled sour cream
6 Tbs. sugar
1 tsp. vanilla extract
½ vanilla bean,
split lengthwise

Instructions

FOR CRUST: Preheat oven to 350°F. Blend graham cracker crumbs and sugar in processor until combine. Gradually add butter and process until moist crumbs form. Press crumbs onto bottom and 1 ½ inches up sides of 10-inch-diameter springform pan with removable bottom. Bake until set, about 12 minutes. Transfer to rack; cool completely. FOR FILLING: Place ½ cup whipping cream in medium bowl; sprinkle gelatin over top. Let stand 5 minutes. Combine 1 cup whipping cream and cream cheese in heavy medium saucepan. Whisk over medium-high heat until mixture is smooth and just beginning to simmer. Remove from heat. Add gelatin mixture; whisk to dissolve. Strain into large bowl. Let stand 45 minutes to cool.Combine remaining 1 ½ cup whipping cream, sour cream, sugar, and vanilla extract in another large bowl. Scrape in seeds from vanilla bean; reserve bean for another use. Using electric mixer, beat until mixture thickens and peaks form. Fold into cream cheese mixture in 3 additions. Transfer filling to prepared crust. Cover and chill until set, at least 6 hours and up to 1 day.

Menu: The Remains of the Day

THE HOLIDAYS

Cranberry Glaze

Ingredients

CRANBERRY TOPPING:
1 Tbs. water
1 tsp. unflavored gelatin
1 cup water (or ruby Port)
1 cup sugar
1 whole star anise
1 cinnamon stick
2 whole cloves
2 2-inch strips orange peel
2 cups fresh cranberries or frozen, thawed

Instructions

FOR CRANBERRY TOPPING: Place 1 Tbs. water in a small bowl. Sprinkle gelatin over. Let stand 5 minutes. Bring water (Port), sugar, star anise, cinnamon stick, cloves, and orange peel to boil in heavy large saucepan over high heat, stirring until sugar dissolves. Reduce heat to medium and simmer 5 minutes. Add cranberries and simmer mixture until cranberries begin to pop, stirring occasionally, about 5 minutes. Remove from heat. Stir some of hot cranberry liquid into gelatin mixture in small bowl to melt gelatin; stir gelatin mixture into cranberry mixture in saucepan. Transfer to medium bowl; refrigerate until cold. (Can be made 1 day head. Cover and keep refrigerated.) Just before serving, remove pan sides to release tart. Cut cheesecake tart into wedges. Spoon cranberry mixture over wedges. Serve.

Menu: The Remains of the Day

HAPPY NEW YEAR

Happy New Year Menu

Southern Comfort Food

Black-Eyed Pea Dip with Pita Chips

Chicken Pot Pie

No-Fuss Blue Cheese and Pear Salad
with Apricot Nectar Dressing

Fluffy Cranberry Mousse

OK, this comfort food is not limited to the South.
However, the black-eyed pea tradition for good luck in the New Year
is, I believe, Southern-African-American. Wherever it came from,
we can use all of the help we can get, so enjoy this dip while watching
the bowl games. Also, you can turn it up a notch with cayenne,
Tabasco, or your personal favorite Scoville unit elevator.

It is also a Southern tradition to have some form of greens on New Year's Day for prosperity in the
coming year.

Lynn's family always had pork roast, greens, Hoppin' John and cornbread. Now you are thinking,
"What (for the love of Pete) is Hoppin' John?" Well, it's black-eyed peas, rice, onions, garlic, hot
peppers and Tobasco to taste.

Now you are going to ask, "Why isn't that our New Year's menu instead of some lame dip and
chicken pot pie?" Because that was what Lynn served at a ladies luncheon to celebrate the New
Year. Fix it and enjoy it – they did.

By the way, if you want Hoppin' John instead, I just gave you the recipe. Ingredient quantities vary
with individual preferences - ad lib.

– Bill

HAPPY NEW YEAR

Black-Eyed Pea Dip with Pita Chips

Ingredients

4 (16 oz.) cans black-eyed peas, drained
2 Tbs. finely chopped onion
1 (4 oz.) can chopped green chilies, drained
3 pickled jalapeño peppers, finely chopped, optional
1 garlic clove, minced
1 tsp. chili powder
1 (8 oz.) package shredded sharp Cheddar cheese
16 Tbs. margarine
Extra shredded sharp Cheddar cheese (optional)

Instructions

Process half of peas, peppers, onions, chilies, garlic and chili powder in a blender until smooth. Microwave cheese and margarine, stirring often, until cheese melts. Stir into black-eyed pea mixture along with other half of black-eyed peas. Pour dip into a chafing dish. Sprinkle with extra cheese. Serve hot with chips. Makes 16 to 20 servings

Southerners eat black-eyed peas on New Year's Day (for good luck) and greens, of some sort, (for prosperity).

Chicken Pot Pie

Ingredients

3 cups butter
2 large onions, chopped
6 celery ribs, chopped
3 cups all-purpose flour
2 (49 oz.) cans chicken broth
5 cups milk
16 cups chopped cooked chicken (about 8 roasted whole chickens)
3 ½ cups sliced carrots, cooked (about 1 lb.)
3 ½ cups green peas, thawed
1 to 2 Tbs. salt
1 Tbs. pepper
2 tsp. hot sauce
1 ½ tsp. poultry seasoning
4 (15 oz.) packages refrigerated piecrusts

Instructions

4 (15 oz.) packages refrigerated piecrusts Divide filling evenly among 4 (15- x 12-inch) disposable aluminum roasting pans.Melt butter in a 4- to 6 gal. stockpot over medium heat; add onions and celery, and sauté until tender.Stir in flour until blended; cook, stirring constantly, 2 minutes. Stir in broth and milk; bring to a boil, and cook, stirring constantly, 2 minutes. Stir in chicken and remaining ingredients.

2 recipes Pot Pie Filling, prepared 1 at a time. Makes 100 ⅔ cup servings.

Menu: Southern Comfort Food

HAPPY NEW YEAR

No-Fuss Blue Cheese and Pear Salad with Apricot Nectar Dressing

Ingredients

½ cup apricot nectar
⅓ cup extra virgin olive oil
⅓ cup white wine vinegar
1 Tbs. Dijon-style mustard
½ tsp. Salt
3 green onions,
finely chopped
½ cup snipped dried apricots
6 ripe red-skinned pears, cored
and cut into wedges
10 cups torn mixed
salad greens (about 9 ozs.)
½ a large head radicchio,
finely shredded (about 2 cups)
8 to 10 oz. blue cheese,
cut into wedges, or goat cheese,
cut into rounds
¾ cup chopped almonds, toasted

Instructions

For Apricot Nectar Dressing, in a very large bowl whisk together apricot nectar, oil, vinegar, mustard, and salt. Stir in green onions and dried apricots. Add pears to dressing and toss to coat. Cover and refrigerate until ready to serve, 30 minutes to 3 ½ hours. When ready to serve, place salad greens on a very large platter. Sprinkle with shredded radicchio. Use a slotted spoon to remove pear wedges from dressing; place pears on radicchio, reserving vinaigrette. Arrange cheese wedges or rounds on the salad, and sprinkle almonds over all. Drizzle with reserved dressing or pass dressing with salad. Makes 12 servings.

Menu: Southern Comfort Food

HAPPY NEW YEAR

Fluffy Cranberry Mousse

Ingredients

½ an 8 oz. pkg. Cream cheese, softened
2 Tbs. sugar
½ tsp. Vanilla
½ cup frozen cranberry juice concentrate, thawed
1 16 oz. can whole cranberry sauce
1 ½ cups whipping cream
1 recipe Sweetened Cranberries (recipe below)

Instructions

1. In a large mixing bowl beat cream cheese with an electric mixer on medium speed for 30 seconds. Beat in sugar and vanilla until smooth. Slowly add cranberry concentrate, beating until very smooth. In a small bowl stir the whole cranberry sauce to remove any large lumps; set aside.

2. In a chilled large mixing bowl beat whipping cream with an electric mixer on low to medium speed until soft peaks form. Fold about half the cranberry sauce and half the whipped cream into the cream cheese mixture until combined. Fold in the remaining cranberry sauce and whipped cream.

3. Serve immediately or cover and refrigerate up to 24 hours (stir before serving if chilled). To serve, spoon fluff into a large serving bowl, 24 chilled demitasse cups, or 12 chilled small dessert dishes. Spoon Sweetened cranberries on top just before serving. Makes 24 (¼ cup) servings or 12 (½ cup) servings.

FROZEN CRANBERRY

FLUFF: Prepare as above through Step 2. Spoon cranberry mixture into 24 freezer-safe demitasse cups or 12 freezer-safe small dessert dishes. Cover and freeze for 24 hours or until firm. To serve, uncover and let stand for 1 to 2 minutes to soften slightly. Top with Sweetened Cranberries.

SWEETENED CRANBERRIES: In a medium skillet combine 1 cup fresh cranberries, ⅓ cup sugar, and 2 Tbs. water. Cook and stir over medium heat until sugar is dissolved and cranberries just begin to pop. Remove from heat. Cover and chill until serving time.

Menu: Southern Comfort Food

TEA PARTY

Girls Having Tea
(Photo by Shain Rievley, Bloom Photography, Knoxville, TN)

The Annual Ladies Tea Event at Northshore Baptist Church, Kirkland, Washington, is an opportunity for the ladies to attend a formal affair that is inconsistent with the Pacific Northwest casual ambiance. A handful of enthusiasts meticulously plan the event starting several months in advance. For several years, Lynn has designed the menu, defined the recipes and managed production of delicacies and savories for about 500 guests. As the ladies are served, she is in fact serving a king - The King and Creator of the Universe.

("…just as you did it unto the least of these, you did it for me." Matthew 25:40.)

TEA PARTY

Tea Party Menu

Tea Specialties

Tomato Aspic with Cucumber

Curried Chicken

Cheddar, Sunflower Seed and Olive

Ham Cornets with Apple Horseradish Filling

Snow Peas with Sesame Dressing

Crab-Artichoke Tarts

Chocolate Cups with Raspberry Mousse

Little Bitty Cakes

Mocha Tartlets

Passion Fruit Tartlets

Angel Kisses

TEA PARTY

Tomato Aspic with Cucumber

Ingredients

5 cups V-8 juice
3 (3 oz.) boxes lemon gelatin
½ cup lime juice
Dash of Worcestershire sauce
Dash hot pepper sauce
30 thin cucumber slices
30 small rounds whole wheat bread
Fresh dill

Instructions

Combine vegetable juice with gelatin and bring to a boil. Stir until dissolved; remove from heat and add lime juice, Worcestershire, and hot sauce. Pour on a cookie sheet which has been prepared with either mayonnaise or cooking spray. Refrigerate until firm. Using a very small heart-shaped cookie cutter cut out small hearts from the congealed aspic. Place a cucumber slice on top of each whole wheat round. Add an aspic heart. Pipe a star of mayonnaise on top and decorate with a tiny piece of dill.

Menu: Tea Specialties

Curried Chicken

Ingredients

2 tsp. curry powder
2 tsp. vegetable oil
¼ tsp. firmly packed light brown sugar
2 tsp. cider vinegar
1 cup minced cooked chicken
¼ cup minced celery
½ cup plus 1 Tbs. mayonnaise
3 Tbs. minced fresh cilantro

Instructions

In a small skillet cook the curry powder in the oil over moderately low heat, stirring, for 3 minutes. Stir in the brown sugar and the vinegar, and let the mixture cool to lukewarm. In a bowl toss together the chicken, the celery, the curry mixture, ½ cup of the mayonnaise, 1 Tbs. of the cilantro, and salt and pepper to taste. The chicken filling may be made up to 1 day in advance and keep covered and chilled. But wait! We have 2 more Tbs. of cilantro! How about sprinkling it on top! A work of beauty.

Menu: Tea Specialties

TEA PARTY

Cheddar, Sunflower Seed and Olive Spread

Ingredients

Instructions

4 oz. cream cheese at room temperature
½ lb. sharp Cheddar, chopped
½ cup pimiento-stuffed green olives, patted dry
⅓ cup coarsely chopped drained bottle pimiento, patted dry
⅓ cup plain yogurt
¼ cup shelled raw sunflower seeds, toasted lightly

In a food processor blend the cream cheese and the Cheddar until the mixture is combine well; add the olives and blend the mixture until the olives are chopped. Add the pimiento and the yogurt and blend the mixture until the pimiento is chopped fine. Add the sunflower seeds and blend the mixture until the seeds are just incorporated, being careful not to purée them. Makes about 2¼ cups.

Menu: Tea Specialties

Ham Cornets with Apple Horseradish Filling

Ingredients

Instructions

2 Granny Smith apples
1 Tbs. fresh lemon juice
¼ tsp. salt
1 ½ Tbs. drained bottled horseradish, or to taste
6 Tbs. sour cream
White pepper to taste
8 thin round slices of Black Forest or Westphalian ham (about ¼ lb.), halved

Peel the apples and grate coarse 1 ½ of them, reserving the remaining apple half in a small bowl of cold water acidulated with the lemon juice. In a sieve toss the grated apple with the salt, let it drain for 10 minutes, and press it gently to remove some of the excess moisture. In a bowl toss the grated apple with the horseradish, the sour cream, and the white pepper. Cut the reserved apple half lengthwise into 16 thin slices and arrange 1 slice in the center of each half slice of ham so that one end of the apple extends slightly beyond the curved edge of the ham. Spoon about 2 tsp. of the filling onto each apple slice and roll the ham into cone shapes. Makes 16 cornets.

Menu: Tea Specialties

TEA PARTY

Snow Peas with Sesame Dressing

Ingredients

1 (7 oz.) pkg. frozen snow peas
Boiling salted water
½ head cauliflower
1 (5 oz.) can water chestnuts, drained and sliced
1 Tbs. pimentos, chopped
SESAME SEED DRESSING
2 Tbs. sesame seeds, toasted
1 Tbs. each: lemon juice, vinegar and sugar
½ tsp. salt
⅓ cup vegetable oil
½ clove garlic, minced or mashed

Instructions

Cook peas in small amount of boiling, salted water until barely tender, about 1 minute. Drain and immediately put in ice water to stop cooking. Separate cauliflower into bite-size clusters, about 2 cups. Cook in boiling, salted water about 3 minutes until tender yet crisp. Drain. Combine peas, cauliflower, water chestnuts and pimentos. Cover and chill. Just before serving, mix with about 3 Tbs. of sesame seed dressing.

To make dressing, place sesame seeds in shallow pan in 350-degree oven for 5-8 minutes or broil (watch closely) until golden brown. Cool. Combine remaining ingredients. Add seeds. Cover and chill. Shake well before serving.

Crab-Artichoke Tarts

Ingredients

2 tsp. all-purpose flour
⅛ tsp. dried whole thyme
⅛ tsp. pepper
1 (4 oz.) carton thawed frozen
egg substitute
or 3 eggs
¼ cup roasted red bell peppers, chopped
1 (14 oz.) can artichoke hearts, drained and chopped
1 (6 oz.) can crabmeat, drained
Vegetable cooking spray
32 (3 ¼ x 3-inch) wonton wrappers
3 Tbs. grated Parmesan cheese
2 Tbs. freeze-dried chives
1 Tbs. butter, melted

Instructions

Combine first 4 ingredients in a bowl; stir well. Add chopped bell peppers, artichokes, and crabmeat; stir well. Coat 32 miniature muffin cups with cooking spray. Gently press 1 wonton wrapper into each muffin cups, allowing ends to extend above edges of cups. Spoon crabmeat mixture evenly into wonton-wrapper cups; sprinkle with cheese and chives. Brush edges of wonton wrappers with melted margarine. Bake at 350°F. for 20 minutes or until crabmeat mixture is set and edges of wonton wrappers are lightly browned. Yield: 32 appetizers.Preparation Time: 25 minutesCooking Time: 20 minutes

Menu: Tea Specialties

TEA PARTY

Chocolate Cups with Raspberry Mousse

Ingredients

18 oz. bittersweet or semisweet chocolate
1 tsp. corn oil
8 (2-inch diameter) aluminum foil baking cups
Non-caloric vegetable cooking spray as needed

Instructions

In the top of a double boiler, melt chocolate with oil over very hot, not boiling, water, blending chocolate and oil. Meanwhile, lightly coat the outside of 8- aluminum foil baking cups with non-caloric vegetable cooking spray. Arrange baking cups upside down, on a baking sheet lined with wax or parchment paper. When chocolate has melted, remove from heat but keep over very hot water. With a pastry brush, carefully "paint" the outside of each baking cups with melted chocolate, including bottom and sides of each. Allow chocolate cups to stand at room temperature, upside-down, until chocolate is firm and sets. Repeat painting process twice more. Allow chocolate " cups" to stand at room temperature for several hours until thoroughly set. Just before serving, carefully loosen the foil baking cups from the inside of the chocolate cups; carefully and gently remove foil cups molds from chocolate cups. Invert chocolate cups right side up, and fill with mousse or other filling as desired. Serve immediately.

Raspberry Mousse

Ingredients

2 cups raspberries, fresh or frozen (may substitute mango, strawberries or kiwi for flavor and color changes)
¼ cup sugar
1 cup whipping cream

Instructions

Puree raspberries in food processor with sugar. Whip cream until stiff. Fold in raspberry puree.

Menu: Tea Specialties

TEA PARTY

Little Bitty Cakes

Ingredients

½ cup butter, softened
1 cup sugar
2 large eggs
1 ½ cups all-purpose flour
1 ½ tsp. baking powder
¼ tsp. salt
½ cup milk
1 tsp. vanilla extract
Faux Fondant
Buttercream Frosting
Candied Flowers
and Raspberries

Instructions

Beat butter at medium speed with an electric mixer until creamy; gradually add sugar, beating well. Add eggs, one at a time, beating until blended after each addition. Combine flour, baking powder, and salt; add to butter mixture alternately with milk, beginning and ending with flour mixture. Stir in vanilla. Spoon into lightly greased miniature muffin pans, filling three-fourths full. Bake at 350°F. for 12 minutes or until golden. Remove from pans; cool on wire racks. Insert a small fork into bottom of a cake, and dip in Faux Fondant, making sure to cover top and sides. Place upright on a wire rack until set. Repeat procedure with remaining cakes and fondant. Spoon Buttercream Frosting into a heavy-duty zip-top plastic bag. Seal. Snip a tiny hole in one corner of bag. Pipe a dollop of frosting onto each cake, and decorate with Candied Flowers and Raspberries. Yield: 3 dozen.

Mocha Tartlets

Ingredients

1 ½ Tbs. cornstarch
¾ cup whole milk
2 oz. fine-quality bittersweet chocolate (not unsweetened), finely chopped
½ Tbs. Tia Maria or other coffee liqueur
½ Tbs. unsalted butter, softened
1 tsp. instant espresso powder

Instructions

Make Custard: Beat together yolks, sugar, cornstarch, and a pinch of salt in a bowl with an electric mixer until thick and pale, about 1 minute. Heat milk in a 2 qt. heavy saucepan over moderate heat until hot but not boiling. Add one third of hot milk to yolk mixture in a slow stream, whisking, then transfer to saucepan. Simmer, whisking constantly, until very thick, 1 ½ to 2 minutes. Remove from heat and add chocolate, liqueur, butter, and espresso powder. Let stand until chocolate is melted, about 1 minute, then whisk until smooth. Force custard through a fine sieve into a bowl. Cover surface of custard with wax paper and chill until cold, at least 4 hours.
COOK'S NOTE: Custard can be made 1 day ahead and chilled, covered. Tartlets can be assembled 2 hours ahead and chilled, covered. Bring to room temperature before serving.

Menu: Tea Specialties

TEA PARTY

Passion Fruit Tartlets

Ingredients

½ cup unsalted butter, melted
¾ cup sugar
2 large eggs, lightly beaten
½ cup passion fruit juices
(see Note)

Instructions

In the top of a double boiler, whisk together the butter, sugar, eggs, and passion fruit juice until the mixture is thick and will hold a line, about 12 minutes. Transfer the double boiler insert to a large bowl filled with ice and cold water, and stir occasionally until cool. The mixture will be quite thick.

Note: Unsweetened passion fruit juice, which is very sour, is sometimes available frozen. Or, in season scoop out and, if desired (it is not necessary), strain the pulp of 1 passion fruit for each 2 Tbs. juice required. If you use regular store bought passion fruit juice, which has been sweetened, add 2 Tbs. of lemon juice for each ½ cup of the juice.Use your favorite pastry recipe for these tartlets.

Angel Kisses

Ingredients

3 egg whites
¾ cup sugar
¼ tsp. cream of tartar
⅛ tsp. peppermint extract
1 cup semisweet chocolate morsels
1 cup chopped pecans
(can omit pecans and add more chocolate)

Instructions

Preheat oven to 325°F. In a medium mixing bowl, beat egg whites until soft peaks. Gradually beat in sugar a little at a time; add cream of tartar and peppermint extract. Beat until stiff peaks form. Fold in chocolate chips and pecans. Drop by teaspoonfuls onto an ungreased baking sheet. Turn off the oven and place the baking sheet inside for 2-3 hours with door closed. If kisses are not dry, reheat oven and dry for 30 minutes, with oven off and the door closed.

Menu: Tea Specialties

My first encounter with Angel Kisses was at a ladies luncheon at the Rashima Family Camp (ARAMCO), Saudi Arabia. OK, it is not a Middle Eastern dessert but sometimes you have to go aound the world to find some of these recipes.

WHERE'S THE BEEF?

National Cattlemen's Association

No organization believes in the future of beef like the National Cattlemen's Association. How many of us are aware of the National Collegiate Beef Quiz Bowl? Teams answer questions about the beef industry including such subjects as physiology, nutrition, reproduction, meat science, current events, etc.

I can imagine it now: "Alex, I'll take cattle reproduction for $50."

The answer: "Rocky Mountain oysters are to Buffalo as these are to cattle."

Response?

... and the game goes on ... if you want to play, contact the National Cattlemen's Association.

Speaking of having a beef with beef, we the consumers must be aware of marketing ploys with the use of the words, "Prime," "Choice," and "Select." A writer for the website, www.primesteakhouses.com says that only 2% of the beef is rated USDA Prime and that lot gets scoffed up by restaurants. "Choice" is the next best and usually your preference from the grocery. However, wordsmiths might use the word choice without reference to the USDA and the meat might actually be USDA Select, ("not far above the bottom of the edible barrel" – according to the same reference).

The rating process is actually rather complex. A beef certifier measures marbling, maturity of the beef, the color of beef and its texture to determine an accurate USDA Grade. For details, read the United States Standards for Grades of Carcass Beef established by the US Department of Agriculture.

Beef is so flexible in choice of formats, it can even be spreadable, either as hamburger in the form of a "Sloppy-Joe," or as an old favorite institutional dining hall meal. I will never forget the cartoon showing a red-faced man with a large grin on his face leaving a friend's home with his very angry wife who said with a pointing finger,

"I don't care what you called it in the Army, it's creamed chipped beef on toast!"

It's time to enjoy a brisket. Let's move on.

– Bill

WHERE'S THE BEEF?

Cattle drive on horseback

Brisket Menu

Brisket of Beef/Pita Bread

Brisket of Beef/Pita Bread

Potato Salad

Green Beans and Mushroom Salad

Frozen Fruit Cups

Chocolate-Hazelnut Blessing Cookies

WHERE'S THE BEEF?

Brisket of Beef/Pita Bread

Ingredients

1 brisket of beef, 2-3 lb.
Garlic salt to salt (or any other seasoning you prefer)
Freshly ground pepper
Sliced onions, if desired
MARINADE:
1 (16 oz.) bottle Italian salad dressing
¼ cup tarragon vinegar, optional
I medium onion, chopped
1 (3 ½ oz.) jar capers, drained
1 (2 oz.) jar pimientos

Instructions

Sprinkle garlic salt and pepper over brisket. Place sliced onions on top. Wrap tightly in foil. Place in tight roasting pan. Cook (300°F. for 4 hours). Chill cooked roast 12 hours or overnight. Slice roast very thin. Mix marinade and pour over meat. Marinate at least 4 hours. Serve cold with pita or other sandwich bread.

Serves 8-10 for dinner or 20 for party

Menu: Brisket of Beef/Pita Bread

A Simple Potato Salad

Ingredients

Potatoes
Celery
Vidalia onion
Hellman's (or Best Foods) mayonnaise
Salt
Pepper, freshly ground
Optional ingredients:
Shredded carrot
Diced red pepper
Olives

Instructions

There are as many recipes for potato salad as there are cooks who make it. When I make a mayonnaise-based potato salad I use the ingredients as listed.

Important: I always add the mayonnaise to the potatoes when they are warm – just enough to bind them together.

Quantities? Make enough for your crowd!

Menu: Brisket of Beef/Pita Bread

WHERE'S THE BEEF?

Green Beans and Mushroom Salad

Ingredients

1 ½ lb. cooked fresh green beans
2 cups fresh mushrooms (chopped)
3 Tbs. shallots, chopped
1 ½ tsp. salt
½ tsp. pepper
½ tsp. dry mustard
½ tsp. paprika
2 oz. tarragon vinegar
1 clove garlic, minced
4 oz. olive oil
¼ cup toasted almonds

Instructions

Combine mushrooms, beans, and shallots.
Combine all other ingredients and pour on top.
Toss with toasted almonds just before serving.

Frozen Fruit Cups

Ingredients

2 cans (20 oz. each) crushed pineapple, undrained
2 packages (10 oz. each) frozen sweetened strawberries, thawed
1 can (20 oz.) fruit cocktail, undrained
1 can (12 oz.) frozen orange juice concentrate, thawed
1 can (6 oz.) frozen lemonade concentrate, thawed
6 medium bananas, cubed

Instructions

In a large bowl combine all ingredients. Pour into foil-lined muffin cups or individual plastic beverage glasses. Freeze until solid. When ready to serve, thaw for 30 - 45 minutes before serving. Yield: 10 servings

Refreshing! This was seved at a tea for 400+ ladies.

Menu: Brisket of Beef/Pita Bread

WHERE'S THE BEEF?

Chocolate-Hazelnut Blessing Cookies

Ingredients

4 large egg whites
1 cup superfine sugar
¾ cup all-purpose flour
¼ cup cocoa powder
Pinch of salt
¼ cup unsalted butter,
melted
3 Tbs. heavy cream
1 tsp. vanilla extract
2 Tbs. hazelnut oil
(available in gourmet and
specialty markets)

Instructions

Heat the oven to 400°F. Whip the egg whites in a mixing bowl with an electric mixer on medium speed. Add the sugar, increase the speed, and mix until smooth. Place the flour, cocoa, and salt into a sifter. Sift into the egg-sugar batter. Continue to mix until well combined. Next add the butter, heavy cream, vanilla extract, and hazelnut oil. Mix again until combined. Spray a cookie sheet with nonstick spray. (I use a nonstick baking mat.) Spoon 1 Tbs. of the batter in 3 places on the cookie sheet (the two lower corners and the upper center). Spread gently with the back of the spoon into 5-inch circles. Bake until slightly crisp at the edges, but still pliable in the center, 6 to 8 minutes. Remove from the oven. Immediately take cookie disks off the tray one at a time (so they stay pliable as you fold the first one). Quickly fold the disk in half, pinching about 2 inches of the top edges together to seal. Immediately take the open loops at each end with your thumb and forefinger of each hand and push inward to from the blessing cookie. Repeat with the next two disks. Then start another batch. When all the cookies are cooled, slip in the blessings. Many will have an easy opening, but for those that don't, fold the blessing tightly and stuff it in a corner of the cookie.

I included scripture verses in these cookies.

Menu: Brisket of Beef/Pita Bread

WHERE'S THE BEEF?

Steak & Ratatouille Menu

Steak with Grilled Ratatouille Salad

Roasted Red Pepper, Artichoke and Black Olive Dip

Chilled Vichyssoise with Cucumber

Grilled Flank Steak

Grilled Ratatouille Salad with Feta Cheese

Raspberry, Strawberry and Orange Granita

Tropical Fruit Fantasy

Roasted Red Pepper, Artichoke and Black Olive Dip

Ingredients

1 can artichokes (14 oz)
1 clove garlic
1 Tbs. balsamic vinegar
2 Tbs. chopped fresh basil
3 chopped green onions
1 ½ cup drained black olives
2 tbs. drained capers
1 cup drained roasted red peppers

Instructions

Finely chop artichoke hearts and garlic in food processor. Add red peppers, olives, green onions, capers and basil and blend until coarse and almost a paste. Add vinegar and blend. Season with salt & pepper.

Menu: Steak with Grilled Ratatouille Salad

WHERE'S THE BEEF?

Chilled Vichyssoise with Cucumber

Ingredients

2 tsp. olive oil
1 cup chopped Vidalia or
other sweet onion
2 garlic cloves, minced
6 ½ cup chopped seeded
peeled English cucumber
(about 3)
3 cups cubed peeled baking
potato (about 1 ¼ pounds)
3 (14-ounce) cans fat-free,
less-sodium chicken broth
3 cups buttermilk
1 Tbs. fresh lemon juice
½ teaspoon salt
¼ teaspoon white pepper
Thinly sliced cucumber

Instructions

Heat oil in a large Dutch oven over medium heat.
Add onion and garlic to pan; cook 8 minutes or
until onion is tender, stirring occasionally.
Add chopped cucumber, potato, and 2 cans broth
to pan; bring to a boil. Cover, reduce heat, and
simmer 20 minutes or until potato is very tender,
stirring occasionally.
Place one-third of potato mixture in a blender.
Remove center piece of blender lid (to allow
steam to escape); secure blender lid on blender.
Place a clean towel over opening in blender lid (to
avoid splatters). Blend until smooth. Pour into a
large bowl. Repeat procedure twice with
remaining potato mixture. Cool.
Add remaining 1 can chicken broth, buttermilk,
juice, salt, and pepper to cooled potato mixture,
stirring well. Cover and chill. Garnish with thinly
sliced cucumber.

Menu: Steak with Grilled Ratatouille Salad

Grilled Flank Steak

Ingredients

1 cup red wine
½ cup olive oil
½ tsp. Worcestershire sauce
2 Tbs. chopped fresh parsley
2 bay leaves
2 green onions, chopped
3 garlic cloves, minced
1 tsp. dried oregano
1 tsp. salt
½ tsp. freshly ground pepper
2 lb. flank steak
Rosemary sprigs
2 Tbs. fresh lemon juice

Instructions

Combine first 10 ingredients. Reserve ⅓ cup red
wine mixture.
Place flank steak in a large shallow dish or large
heavy-duty zip-top plastic bag. Pour red wine
mixture over steak. Cover or seal, and chill 2 to 4
hours, turning occasionally.
Remove flank steak from marinade, discarding
marinade.
Grill, covered with grill lid, over medium-high heat
for 8 to 10 minutes on each side or to desired
degree of doneness, brushing with reserved wine
mixture using rosemary sprigs as the brush. Cut
steak diagonally across the grain into thin strips.
Squeeze juice over steak before serving.

Menu: Steak with Grilled Ratatouille Salad

WHERE'S THE BEEF?

Grilled Ratatouille Salad with Feta Cheese

Ingredients

1 (12 to 14 oz.) eggplant, cut into ½-inch-thick rounds
1 zucchini, quartered lengthwise
1 red bell pepper, cut lengthwise into 6 strips
1 medium onion, cut into ½-inch-thick rounds
3 Tbs. purchased garlic-flavored olive oil
2 to 3 tsp. balsamic vinegar
⅔ cup crumbled feta cheese
2 Tbs. slivered fresh basil

Instructions

Prepare barbecue (medium-high heat). Place eggplant, zucchini, red bell pepper and onion on baking sheet. Drizzle with oil and sprinkle with salt and pepper, turn to coat. Grill bell red pepper and onion fo 4 minutes. Then add eggplant and zucchini and grill all for another 6 minutes. Divide vegetables between 2 plates; drizzle with vinegar. Sprinkle cheese and basil over and serve. Makes 2 servings; can be doubled.

Raspberry, Strawberry and Orange Granita

Ingredients

1 cup orange juice
¾ cup water
½ cup honey
¼ cup sugar
1 tsp. grated orange peel
1 16 oz. package fresh strawberries, hulled, quartered (about 3 ½ cups)
2 ½ pt. baskets fresh raspberries

Instructions

Combine orange juice, ¾ cup water, honey, sugar and orange peel in blender. Add half of strawberries and half of raspberry puree until almost smooth. Add remaining berries; puree until smooth. Pour mixture out onto 13x9x2-inch baking pan. Freeze until edges are icy and center Is slushy, about 1 hour 30 minutes. Stir icy edges into slushy center. Freeze granita until solid, stirring every 45 minutes, about 3½ hours longer. Using fork, scrape granita down length of pan, forming icy flakes. Cover and freeze at least 1 hour and up to 2 days. Spoon granita into glasses. Calories per serving 135; no fat, no cholesterol.
Makes 8 servings.

Menu: Steak with Grilled Ratatouille Salad

GREAT SALADS

Why Are Salads So Popular?

Popularity doesn't always mean you can dance or make great conversation. A salad can do neither and yet its popularity is exceptional. There are at least 35 salads in this book!

Ladies enjoying salads

The Salad

A small side salad in a bowl,
Served mainly to console
The expectant guest - it's a major ordeal
If it isn't served before the meal.
Then the salad grew in scope and size
And before we could realize,
What once was considered rabbit food,
We now were expected to construe,
As our main course - a new entree
To stick to our ribs throughout the day,
Served at noon for us to munch,
The salad has taken over lunch.

Many people associate "low calorie" with the word, "salad." What once might have been served as a meat with vegetables and a side salad is now mixed-up on a plate or in a bowl and called a salad entree.

Then, how would you define a salad?

I would say that a salad is an assortment of foods, cut up, mixed together with a dressing.

What if one of the foods is left out?

It's still a salad.

I guess a salad is pretty easy to make, huh?

That's why they are so popular.

– Bill

GREAT SALADS

Anyone can mix up a salad. Having catered a ladies monthly luncheon for 13 years, I have a wealth of salad recipes. There are enough chicken salad recipes to do a cookbook of that topic alone! Most of us can find enough ingredients in our refrigerator and cupboard to pull together a salad. (That is, unless we eat from vending machines.)

DON'T HESITATE TO MAKE YOUR OWN DRESSING! It's easy to do and you can avoid the preservatives found in commercial brands.

– Lynn

Note that there are salads scattered though out this book and all are Great Salads. The Chicken Tortellini is a good leadoff menu in this Great Salad section.

Chicken Tortellini Menu

Chicken Tortellini Salad

Chicken Tortellini Salad

Foccacia

Italian Love Cake

GREAT SALADS

Chicken Tortellini Salad

Ingredients

1 box Parmesan cheese-filled
tortellini (½ lb.)
3 whole boneless chicken
breasts cooked, then shredded
1 small bunch broccoli, steamed
lightly, then cut into florets and
pieces
1 small can of pitted black
olives, sliced
½ red pepper (roasted if
possible), sliced thin
½ lb. (about 16) snow pea pods
steamed slightly and cut into
thirds.
Can also add ripe tomato, baby
corn, sliced scallions, water
chestnuts, etc.
1 bottle Girard's Romano
Cheese dressing or other Italian-
style dressing

Instructions

Cook the pasta according to directions (about 18 minutes for al dente). Rinse under cold water and drain well. Add the other ingredients and mix with dressing. Fresh grated Romano cheese is good to add, as is freshly ground black pepper. No salt! To roast a red pepper: Place aluminum foil on a cookie sheet and oil slightly (I use a spray oil.). Place firm, thick-walled red peppers on pan and place under broiler (close as possible). As the skins blacken, turn with long tongs until entire pepper is charred. (Don't worry, the inside is OK.). Remove with tongs to a Tupperware container with lid. Allow to cool. Slip charred skins off peppers; remove seeds and slice lengthwise into strips. Store in glass jar covered with a tablespoon of red wine vinegar and olive oil (or covered with a tablespoon of red wine vinegar and olive oil (or covered with Girard's dressing). Keeps up to a month in refrigerator. This is good on sandwiches, in salads, on cheese, with grilled meats, etc.

Foccacia

Ingredients

1-½ cup warm water
2 Tbs. olive oil
2 tsp. salt
4¼ cups all-purpose flour
2 tsp. sugar
2 tsp. yeast

Instructions

This dough can be made in a bread maker.Pat recipe of pizza dough about ½ inch thick onto a baking sheet (round or rectangular) dusted with flour or cornmeal. Dimple dough with fingertips.Brush with olive oil and sprinkle with fresh herbs (rosemary, oregano, or basil), Parmesan or Romano cheese, black pepper and salt. Let dough rise 15-20 minutes. Place in a preheated 400°F. oven until golden brown. Remove. Let cool 5 minutes. Cut into squares or wedges depending on shape of pan. Great as breadsticks with meal or as bread or sandwich.

Menu: Chicken Tortellini Salad

GREAT SALADS

Italian Love Cake

Ingredients

1 box Duncan Hines Moist Deluxe White Cake Mix (or your favorite white cake recipe)

1 tsp. Almond flavoring

3 oz. semisweet (or dark) chocolate chips

1 30 oz. container ricotta cheese

¼ cup sugar

4 eggs

1 tsp. vanilla or almond flavoring

1 box (3 ¾ oz.) instant chocolate pudding

1 cup milk

1 carton (8 oz.) whipped topping

Instructions

Mix cake as directed on box. To the mix, I added 1 tsp. almond flavoring In the top of a double boiler set over simmering water, melt the 3 oz. of semisweet chocolate. Remove from heat and stir until smooth. Set aside to cool. After preparing batter, pour half of the batter into a bowl. Stir the chocolate into the batter, blending well. Put the batter into a greased and floured 9 x 13-inch pan by alternating spoons of vanilla batter and chocolate batter. With a table knife, gently draw swirls through the batter to marbleize it slightly (don't touch pan bottom or sides with knife). In a separate bowl, combine ricotta, sugar, eggs and vanilla; mix well. Spoon over top of unbaked cake. Bake at 350°F. for 1 hour. Cool. Mix pudding with milk; fold in whipped topping. Spread over cake; refrigerate.

You can cut the calorie/fat content of this recipe by using low-fat ricotta, milk, chocolate pudding and whipped topping.

Menu: Chicken Tortellini Salad

GREAT SALADS

Paella Salad Menu

Paella Salad

Paella Salad

Spinach Salad with Feta, Mint and Olives

Parmesan Twists

Hat Cookies and Fresh Fruit Cups

Creative Paella Artist

GREAT SALADS

Paella Salad

Ingredients

1 pkg. (6 oz.) saffron rice
2 Tbs. tarragon vinegar
⅓ cup vegetable oil
⅛ tsp. salt
¼ tsp. dry mustard
2 ½ cups diced cooked
chicken
1 tomato, peeled and chopped
1 green pepper, chopped
1 cup shrimp (optional)
½ cup green peas, cooked
¼ cup minced onion
⅓ cup sliced celery
1 Tbs. chopped pimento
Additional ingredients: artichoke
hearts, sausage,
other seafood, etc.

Instructions

Cook rice according to package directions. Mix vinegar, oil, salt, and mustard. Pour this over cooked rice. Let stand at room temperature until cool. Add remaining ingredients and toss well. Chill at least 2 or 3 hours. Serves 6.

Spinach Salad with Feta, Mint and Olives

Ingredients

⅓ cup extra-virgin olive oil
2 Tbs. rice wine vinegar
¼ tsp. freshly ground black
pepper
⅓ cup thinly sliced
purple onion
6 Calamata olives
Croutons
2 large cloves garlic, minced
⅛ tsp. salt
6 cups fresh torn
spinach leaves
2 oz. feta cheese, crumbled
½ tsp finely chopped
fresh mint

Instructions

Whisk together oil, garlic, vinegar, salt, and pepper. Toss dressing spinach and next 4 ingredients. Garnish with croutons, if desired. Serves 6.

Menu: Paella Salad

GREAT SALADS

Brown Derby Menu

Brown Derby Cobb Salad

Brown Derby Cobb Salad

Rolls/Butter

Molasses Cookie Baskets

Apple Blackberry Sorbet

Gingered Fresh Fruit

What does this have to do with the well known Brown Derby and The Brown Derby Cookbook? According to our source, it was there that the first Cobb salad recipe was printed. If it is a Cobb salad it must be made of cobs. No, that is not the case. Instead it is named for its creator, Bob Cobb, owner of the Brown Derby in the mid-1930's. Did Lynn use the same recipe in this book? I don't know, she got it from the American Century Cookbook along with the Brown Derby French Dressing.

– Bill

GREAT SALADS

Brown Derby Cobb Salad

Ingredients

4 cups finely cut iceberg lettuce (about ½ head)
2 cups finely cut watercress (about ½ bunch)
5 cups finely cut chicory (about 1 small bunch)
4 cups finely cut romaine (about ½ head)
2 medium vine-ripe tomatoes, peeled and cored
2 cooked chicken breasts (about 1 lb.) roasted, boned
6 strips bacon, crisply cooked
1 medium avocado, halved, pitted, and peeled
3 hard-cooked eggs, peeled and finely chopped
2 Tbs. snipped fresh chives
½ cup finely grated (or crumbled) Roquefort cheese

Instructions

Arrange iceberg lettuce, watercress, chicory, and romaine in artful clumps in large shallow salad bowl or deep platter. Halve tomatoes, seed, cut into fine dice, and arrange in strips across middle of greens. Dice chicken and arrange on top of greens. Crumble or chop bacon fine and sprinkle over salad. Finely dice avocado and wreathe around edge of salad. Decorate with hard-cooked eggs, chives, and Roquefort. Just before serving, add 1 cup dressing, bring to the table, and toss well in front of guests.

Note: For large crowds I serve dressing in individual cups. Soggy greens are a no-no!

Brown Derby French Dressing

Ingredients

¼ cup water (optional)
¾ cup red wine vinegar
1 tsp. sugar
Juice of ½ small lemon
¾ tsp. salt (or to taste)
1 tsp. black pepper
1 Tbs. Worcestershire sauce
1 tsp. dry English mustard
1 clove garlic, peeled and minced
1 cup olive oil
1 cup vegetable oil

Instructions

Shake water (if using), vinegar, sugar, lemon juice, salt, pepper, Worcestershire, and garlic in 1 qt. shaker jar. Add olive and vegetable oils and shake well. Taste for salt and pepper and adjust as needed. Cover tightly and store in refrigerator. Shake well before using.

See the commentary about the source on the previous page.

GREAT SALADS

Molasses Cookie Baskets

Ingredients

¼ cup unsalted butter
¼ cup sugar
¼ cup light unsulfured molasses
½ tsp. grated lemon peel
½ tsp. ground ginger
1 tsp. vanilla extract
½ cup all-purpose flour, sifted

Instructions

Preheat oven to 325°F. Butter 2 large nonstick cookie sheets. Bring first 5 ingredients to simmer in heavy small saucepan over medium heat stirring constantly. Remove from heat. Whisk in vanilla, then flour. Drop mixture by level tablespoonfuls onto cookie sheets spacing 6 inches apart and forming 3 cookies on each sheet. Using buttered fingertips, press out each round to 4 ½-inch diameters. Bake 1 sheet until cookies are deep brown, about 10-12 minutes. Cool cookies on sheet just until firm enough to lift without breaking, about 2 minutes. Working quickly, lift 1 cookie from sheet. Drape cookie topside up over inverted ¾ cup custard dish. Gently flatten cookie on dish bottom; crimp sides to form fluted cups. Repeat with remaining 2 cookies, returning cookie sheet to oven briefly if cookies harden. Repeat baking and molding process with remaining cookies. Cool. Gently remove cookies from dishes.

Gingered Fresh Fruit

Ingredients

½ cup sugar
½ cup water
¼ cup minced crystallized ginger
1 (1 pt.) basket strawberries, hulled, quartered
1 (½ pt.) basket blueberries
2 peaches, peeled, pitted, sliced
2 pt. purchased sorbet

Instructions

Stir first 3 ingredients in heavy small saucepan over medium heat until sugar dissolves. Increase heat and boil 3 minutes. Refrigerate ginger syrup until cold. (Cookies and syrup can be prepared 1 week ahead. Store cookies at room temperature in airtight container. Keep sauce refrigerated.) Place fruit in bowl. Add half of ginger syrup and toss well. Place 1 cookie on each of 6 plates. Fill each with 3 scoops of sorbet and spoon fruit and remaining syrup over.

Menu: Brown Derby Cobb Salad

GREAT SALADS

Chinese Chicken Menu

Chinese Chicken Salad

Chinese Chicken Salad

Hawaiian Delight

Chinese Chicken Salad

Ingredients

DRESSING:
2 tsp. olive oil
1 Tbs. chopped shallots
2 Tbs. Dry white wine
1 (16 oz.) bottle any Asian
sesame-ginger dressing
2 Tbs. Sesane toasted seeds
WONTON CHIPS:
Peanut oil, for deep-frying
10 (3-inch-square) wonton skins,
cut into ¼-inch-wide strips
SALAD:
1 lb. boneless, skinless chicken
breast halves
1 red bell pepper, seeded and
julienned
⅓ cup sliced water chestnuts
5 cups mixed salad greens
½ cup shredded coconut, toasted
½ cup dry-roasted peanuts
½ cup raisins

Instructions

Prepare a fire in a charcoal grill, or preheat a gas grill.To prepare the dressing, in a skillet, heat the olive oil over medium heat. Add the shallots and sauté for 3 minutes, until translucent. Add the wine, chutney, and bottled dressing and heat through. Add the sesame seeds. Allow to cool. (Today, the chutney and bottled dressing were heated through, and then the sesame seeds were added.) To prepare the wonton chips, in a saucepan, pour in the oil to a depth of 2 inches and heat to 350°F. Add the wonton strips to the oil, a few at a time. They will fry very fast, taking only about 15 seconds to get crispy. Using a slotted spoon, transfer to paper towels to drain. Place the chicken on the grill rack and grill, turning as needed, for 10 to 20 minutes, until done. Cut into strips and allow to cool.In a bowl, combine the chicken strips, bell pepper, and water chestnuts. Add ½ cup of the dressing to coat the mixture.In another bowl, toss the salad greens lightly with ½ cup of the dressing. (The remaining dressing can be stored for up to 30 days in an airtight container in the refrigerator.) Divide the greens among 6 plates, and top each with one-sixth of the chicken mixture. Sprinkle each salad with the coconut, peanuts, raisins, and wonton chips. Serve immediately.

Menu: Chinese Chicken Salad

GREAT SALADS

Hawaiian Delight

Ingredients

CRUST:
9 Tbs. butter, softened
½ cup sugar
1 tsp. vanilla extract
1 ½ cups all-purpose flour
⅛ tsp. salt
Cooking spray
FILLING:
2 (11 oz.) cans mandarin
oranges in light syrup,
undrained
¼ cup sugar
1 (16 oz.) carton fat-free sour
cream
1 (8 oz.) carton low-fat sour
cream
2 (3.4 oz.) packages vanilla
instant pudding mix or
2 (1.4 oz.) packages sugar-free
vanilla instant pudding mix
1 (8 oz.) container frozen
reduced-calorie whipped
topping, thawed
Mint sprigs (optional)

Menu: Chinese Chicken Salad

Instructions

To prepare crust, combine the butter, ½ cup sugar, and vanilla in a large bowl. Beat at medium speed of a mixer until light and fluffy (about 2 minutes). Lightly spoon flour into dry measuring cups; level with a knife. Add flour and salt to butter mixture, beating at low speed until well blended.Preheat oven to 400°F. Pat dough into a 13 x 9-inch baking dish coated with cooking spray, and pierce bottom of dough with a fork. Bake at 400°F. for 12 minutes or until lightly browned. Cool crust on a wire rack.To prepare filling, drain mandarin oranges over a large bowl, reserving ½ cup juice. Combine juice, ¼ cup sugar, sour creams, and pudding mix in a large bowl. Stir in the orange segments. Spoon orange mixture over crust, spreading evenly. Top with whipped topping. Chill 1 hour. Garnish with mint, if desired. Yield: 16 servings.

GREAT SALADS

April Salad Menu

April Salad with Strawberry Dressing

Sunny Spring Lemonade

An April Salad with Strawberry Dressing

Petite Croissants with Savory Whipped Butter Spread

Snickerdoodles

Sunny Spring Lemonade

Ingredients

6 cups white grape juice, chilled

1 (12 oz.) can frozen lemonade concentrate, thawed and undiluted

5 ½ cups club soda, chilled

Instructions

Stir together all ingredients in a 1 gal. pitcher or punch bowl. Serve over ice. Yield: 3 qt..

Menu: April Salad with Strawberry Dressing

GREAT SALADS

An April Salad with Strawberry Dressing
Ingredients   Instructions

1 bag cut-up romaine lettuce
1 bag cut-up mixed baby lettuces   Make certain that the chicken breasts are
    and salad greens   cooked, then, mix up the ingredients and apply
4 boneless, skinless chicken   the dressing.
    breasts, cooked
6 oz. crumbled feta cheese
½ cup strawberries, cut into
    halves or quarters
½ cup raspberries
½ cup blueberries
½ cup boysenberries (or
    blackberries)
½ cup cashew nuts
1 can (6 oz.) mandarin oranges,
    drained
1 cup mushroom pieces

Menu: April Salad with Strawberry Dressing

Strawberry Dressing
Ingredients   Instructions

½ cup buttermilk   In blender or food processor container, add all
1 cup fresh strawberries,   dressing ingredients.Cover and process until
    sliced   mixture is smooth.
2 tsp. honey
¼ tsp. allspice

Menu: April Salad with Strawberry Dressing

GREAT SALADS

Petite Croissants with Savory Whipped Butter Spread

Ingredients

1 ½ cups butter, softened
½ cup spicy brown mustard
1 cup finely chopped pecans, toasted

Instructions

Stir together first 3 ingredients. Spread on petite croissants.

Snickerdoodles

Ingredients

1 cup butter
1½ cups sugar
2 eggs
2 ¾ cups sifted flour
2 tsp. cream of tartar
1 tsp. baking soda
1 tsp. salt
2 Tbs. sugar
2 tsp. cinnamon

Instructions

A Pacific Northwest Favorite!
Pre-heat oven to 400°F. In a large bowl combine the butter, sugar and eggs; mix thoroughly with electric mixer on medium speed until well blended, (1-2 minutes). Sift together flour, cream of tartar, baking soda and salt and stir into butter mixture. In a small bowl stir together the remaining sugar and cinnamon. Shape dough into 1½ inch balls, (1 Tbs. per ball), and roll out in cinnamon sugar. Arrange dough balls 2 inches apart on ungreased cookie sheets. Bake 8-10 minutes until edges are set but centers are still soft.

Menu: April Salad with Strawberry Dressing

GREAT SALADS

Chef's Salad Menu

Chef's Salad

Chef's Salad

Lemon Ice Box Pie

Chef's Salad

Ingredients

8 cups salad greens, washed/ torn into bite-sized pieces
1 cup ham, julienne strips
1 cup turkey, julienne strips
½ cup green onion, chopped fine
½ cup celery, chopped fine
1 cup cherry or grape tomatoes, halved
½ cup cheddar cheese, julienne strips
2 eggs, hard-boiled, peeled and sliced
¼ cup bacon bits, for garnish
8 oz. salad dressing, of your choice

Instructions

Prepare salad greens of your choice by washing and tearing them into bite-sized pieces; place in a large bowl. Toss the greens with remaining ingredients, reserving some julienned pieces of meat and cheese for garnish. Just before serving, toss with a dressing of your choice and garnish with strips of meat, cheese and hard-cooked egg slices. Serve salad with crusty bread, rolls or bread sticks. Serves 4.

GREAT SALADS

Lemon Ice Box Pie

Ingredients

1 (6 oz.) carton
whipped topping
1 (6 oz.)can frozen lemonade
concentrate, thawed
1 14 oz. can sweetened
condensed milk
1 prepared graham
cracker crust

Instructions

In a large bowl, combine the topping, lemonade concentrate, and condensed milk, and beat using an electric mixer. Pour into the pie shell and chill for 1 hour before serving. Frozen limeade concentrate may be used in place of lemonade for a lime pie. Yield: 6 servings.

Menu: Chef's Salad

SPECIALTIES

Lynn: *"Why did you name this section, Specialties?"*

Bill: *"Because they didn't seem to fit anywhere else."*

Lynn: *"But why are they special?"*

Bill: *"Everything that you serve is special."*

Lynn: *"hummm, ok."*

Specialty Rice & Artichoke Pie Menu

Rice and Artichoke Pie

Rice and Artichoke Pie

Mandarin Spinach Salad
with French Dressing

Pumpkin Muffins
with Orange Cream Cheese

Apple Crisp

SPECIALTIES

Rice and Artichoke Pie

Ingredients

Instructions

1 package Herb and Butter Rice-A-Roni

1 cup chopped ham or 2 Italian sausages, browned and crumbled

4 medium artichokes, cleaned, trimmed and cooked (or 1 can)

1 cup shredded Swiss cheese

3 green onions, chopped

¼ cup chopped green pepper

4 large eggs, beaten

1 cup milk

¼ tsp. Salt

Dash of pepper

6 to 8 Servings

Cook rice according to package directions. Cool. Preheat oven to 350°F. Press rice onto bottom and sides of buttered, deep 10-inch pie plate. Sprinkle with ham or sausage. Remove all outside leaves from artichokes. Cut artichokes, including bottoms, into 1-inch pieces. Place on top of meat. Sprinkle evenly with cheese, onions, and green pepper. Combine eggs, milk, salt and pepper. Pour over pie. Bake, uncovered, about 50 minutes, or until egg mixture is firm. Cool slightly and cut into wedges.May be made in advance and refrigerated before cooking. Bring to room temperature prior to baking. NOTE: Can add additional vegetables to this (i.e. celery, carrots, mushrooms, zucchini, summer squash, green beans, broccoli, cauliflower, etc.)

Menu: Rice and Artichoke Pie

SPECIALTIES

Mandarin Spinach Salad with French Dressing

Ingredients

1 (1 lb.) bag fresh spinach
½ lb. fresh mushrooms, washed
1 (11 oz.) can mandarin orange sections
1 bunch spring onions, sliced (bottoms only)
Salt and freshly ground pepper, to taste
4-5 slices bacon fried and crumbled
French Dressing (Recipe below)

Instructions

Prepare spinach for salad. Chill. To serve, add orange sections, onions, bacon, mushrooms and seasonings. Toss with French dressing. Serves 4-6.

French Dressing

Ingredients

¾ tsp. dry mustard
½ tsp. black pepper
½ tsp. paprika
½ tsp. sugar
2 oz. cider vinegar
6 oz. salad oil

Instructions

Combine all ingredients. Shake. Chill. Yield: ¾ cup.

Menu: Rice and Artichoke Pie

SPECIALTIES

Pumpkin Muffins with Orange Cream Cheese

Ingredients

2 ½ cups unbleached
white flour
2 tsp. baking powder
2 tsp. baking soda
⅛ tsp. salt
⅓ cup dark brown sugar
¼ tsp. ground cloves
½ tsp. ground cinnamon
¼ tsp. freshly grated nutmeg
1-½ cups pureed fresh or
canned pumpkin
2 eggs
1 Tbs. vegetable oil

Instructions

Preheat oven to 400°F. If you're not using nonstick muffin tins, lightly oil and flour 12 muffin tins.In a large mixing bowl, combine the flour, baking power, baking soda, and salt.In another bowl, combine the remaining ingredients, whisking until smooth. Combine the dry and wet ingredients, beating lightly with a wooden spoon. Divide the batter among the prepared muffin tins and bake in the center of the oven for 15 to 18 minutes or until the tops are lightly browned and a toothpick inserted in the center comes out clean. Allow the muffins to sit in the muffin tins for 5 minutes, then remove and serve immediately. Makes 12. NOTE: The muffins are best right from the oven. Reheat them, covered in foil, in a 300°F. oven for 10 minutes. They can also be frozen for a few months in an airtight plastic bag or heavily wrapped in foil.

NOTE: Spread for muffins was made from fresh orange zest and a little sugar mixed into creamed cheese.

Apple Crisp

Ingredients

6 crisp sour apples
1 cup flour
1 cup brown sugar
¼ lb. butter

Instructions

Pare, core and slice apples, and put in pie plate. Mix flour and brown sugar, then add butter and mix until crumbly. Sprinkle this mixture over apples and bake at 350°F. for about 30 minutes or until apples are done. Serve warm with ice cream or whipped topping.

NOTE: Served with whipped topping mixed with cinnamon.

Menu: Rice and Artichoke Pie

SPECIALTIES

Tomato Pie Menu

Savory Fresh Tomato Pie
Peach Iced Tea

Savory Fresh Tomato Pie

Marinated Green Beans and Roasted Red Peppers

Summer Fruit Salad with Blueberry Vinaigrette

Bread Sticks

Fresh Fruit Cups with Blackberry Sauce

Warm Blackberry Pie Sundaes

You will love the tomato pie. People who have had it request it repeatedly.

SPECIALTIES

Peach Iced Tea

Ingredients

3 (11.5 oz.) cans peach
nectar
2 qt. brewed tea
1 cup sugar
¼ cup fresh lemon juice

Instructions

Stir together all ingredients; chill until ready to serve.
Makes about ¾ gal.

Savory Fresh Tomato Pie

Ingredients

1 9-inch piecrust of your choice
¾ cup all-purpose flour
½ tsp. salt
¼ tsp. pepper
½ tsp. Italian seasoning
4 medium sliced tomatoes
5 green onions
¼ cup fresh basil leaves,
chopped, or 1 tsp. dried basil
¾ cup Best Foods mayonnaise
1 ½ cups shredded Monterey
Jack cheese
Garnish: fresh basil sprigs

Instructions

Combine flour and next 4 ingredients in a zip-top
plastic bag and shake to coat. Arrange tomato slices
in piecrust; sprinkle with green onions and fresh
basil.Combine mayonnaise and cheese and spread
over peeled and sliced tomatoes. Shield edges with
strips of aluminum foil to prevent excessive
browning.Bake at 375°F. for 25 minutes. Garnish, if
desires. Makes 6-8 servings.

NOTE: You can substitute yogurt or half yogurt/half
mayonnaise for the mayonnaise.

Use your imagination and try different vegetables in
the pie.

Menu: Savory Fresh Tomato Pie

SPECIALTIES

Basil-Garlic Tart Pastry

Ingredients

⅓ cup fresh basil leaves
1 medium garlic clove
1¼ cups unbleached
all-purpose flour
½ tsp. kosher salt
8 Tbs. (1 stick)
unsalted butter,
chilled and cut into
8 to 10 pieces
4-5 Tbs. ice water

Instructions

Place the basil and garlic in the work bowl of a food processor. Process, scraping down the sides of the bowl as needed, until finely chopped. Add flour and salt; pulse to combine.

Add butter. Pulse about 10 times, or until the mixture resembles pea-sized crumbs.

Add water, 1 Tbs. at a time, pulsing several times after each addition. After 4 Tbs. water have been added, process the dough for several seconds to see if the mixture forms a ball. If not, add remaining water. Process until dough forms into a ball. Remove dough from processor. Flatten the dough into a 5-inch disk. Wrap it in plastic, and refrigerate for at least 1 hour. (The dough can be placed in a zipper-lock plastic bag and refrigerated for several days or frozen for 1 month. If frozen, defrost the dough in the refrigerator.) Roll out the dough on a lightly floured surface into a 12-inch circle. Lay the dough over the tart pan, and press it into the pan. Trim the dough, and proceed with the recipe as directed.

Marinated Green Beans and Roasted Red Peppers

Ingredients

3 large red bell peppers
2 lb. slender green beans,
trimmed
¾ cup olive oil
⅓ cup red wine vinegar
3 garlic cloves, minced

Instructions

Char peppers over gas flame or in broiler until blackened on all sides. Enclose in Ziploc bag and let stand 10 minutes. Peel and seed peppers. Cut into ½-inch-wide strips. Transfer to a large bowl. Cook beans in large pot of boiling salted water until crisp-tender, about 5 minutes. Drain. Transfer to bowl of ice water to cool. Drain well. Add to bowl with peppers. Whisk oil, vinegar and garlic in small bowl to blend well. Pour over vegetables, season to taste with salt and pepper. Cover, chill up to 6 hours. Serves 12 to 14.

Menu: Savory Fresh Tomato Pie

SPECIALTIES

Summer Fruit Salad with Blueberry Vinaigrette

Ingredients   Instructions

2 cups fresh or frozen   Summer Fruit-Chicken Salad with Blueberry
blueberries   Vinaigrette: Add 2 cups chopped cooked chicken to
1 cup fresh strawberries halved   serve as a main dish.
2 nectarines, sliced
8 cups mixed salad greens
Blueberry Vinaigrette
½ cup slivered almonds,
toasted (optional)

Menu: Savory Fresh Tomato Pie

Blueberry Vinaigrette

Ingredients   Instructions

1 ½ cup olive or light nut seed oil   Puree all ingredients in blender. Store in a jar in
1 cup blueberries (frozen ok)   the refrigerator for up to 4 weeks.In stainless steel
¼ cup cider vinegar   saucepan combine 1 ½ cups berries with rice
¼ cup lime juice   vinegar. Bring to a boil; reduce heat. Simmer 3
1 tsp. mustard seed   minutes. Stir in honey. Remove from heat. Pour
Salt and pepper to taste   mixture through a fine mesh strainer into bowl.
                                 Discard berries.Transfer liquid to clean jar or
                                 bottle. Add remaining berries. Cover tightly with
                                 non-metallic lid (or use plastic wrap between jar
                                 and lid). Store in a cool, dark place for up to 6
                                 months.

Menu: Savory Fresh Tomato Pie

SPECIALTIES

Blackberry Sauce

Ingredients

4 ½ pt. baskets fresh blackberries
(about 5 ½ cups)
1 cup orange juice
¾ cup sugar
2 tsp. grated orange peel
¼ tsp. ground cinnamon

Instructions

Combine 4 cups blackberries, orange juice, sugar, orange peel, and cinnamon in medium saucepan. Bring to a boil. Reduce heat to low; simmer until berries are soft and begin to release juices, about 8 minutes. Transfer 2 cups berry mixture to processor; puree until almost smooth. Return mixture to same saucepan. Stir in remaining blackberries. (Can be made 2 hours ahead. Let stand at room temperature. Re-warm berry mixture over medium heat until just warm before continuing.)

Note: For mostt luncheons I serve a fruit alternative for dessert. For example, drizzle the blackberry sauce over a cup of seasonal fresh fruit. (It was also drizzled over ice cream with butter cookies on the side – so much for the fruit alternative, huh?)

Warm Blackberry Pie Sundaes

Ingredients

1 ½ qt. vanilla ice cream
1 (7-8oz. package shortbread cookies (such as, Pepperidge Farm Chessmen), crumbled
(about 2 cups)
Blackberry Sauce

Instructions

Divide crumbs among 8 goblets or bowls. Add 1 scoop ice cream and spoon the warm blackberry sauce over. Serve.

Menu: Savory Fresh Tomato Pie

SPECIALTIES

Cheesy Chicken Quiche Menu

Cheesy Chicken and Asparagus Quiche

An Island Punch

Cheesy Chicken and Asparagus Quiche

Spring Salad with Strawberries
and Lemon-Poppy Seed Dressing

Yeast Rolls with Dill Butter

Lemon Bisque

An Island Punch

Ingredients

3 (6 oz.) cans
frozen pineapple juice
concentrate
1 (6 oz.) can frozen orange
juice concentrate
1 (6 oz.) can frozen
lemonade concentrate,
3 qt. cold wate
1 cup chilled strong tea
2 (32 oz.) bottles
chilled ginger ale

Instructions

In a large punch bowl combine the thawed
ingredients and add ice cubes or ice ring. Makes 50
(½ cup) servings.

Menu: Cheesy Chicken and Asparagus Quiche

SPECIALTIES

Lynn Wolter

SPECIALTIES

Cheesy Chicken and Asparagus Quiche

Ingredients

1- 9" piecrust
2 Tbs. butter
2 Tbs. olive oil
3 cloves garlic minced
1 cup chopped onion
1 cup chopped asparagus
(1-inch pieces)
2 boneless/skinless chicken
breasts, diced
3 large eggs
1 cup half-and-half
1 tsp. dry mustard
½ tsp. salt
¼ tsp. black pepper
1 ½ cups grated
Monterey Jack cheese

Instructions

Preheat oven to 450°F. Bake piecrust 6 to 8 minutes. Reduce heat to 375F. In a large skillet, melt butter and olive oil over medium-high heat. Sauté garlic, onion, and asparagus 3 to 5 minutes, or until tender. With a slotted spoon, remove vegetables to another bowl, leaving as much oil in pan as possible. Add chicken to pan and cook 5 to 7 minutes, or until lightly browned; remove from pan and set aside. In a small bowl, whisk together eggs, half-and-half, mustard, salt, and pepper. To assemble quiche, sprinkle 1 cup cheese over bottom of prepared crust. Layer chicken and vegetable mixture on top of cheese. Pour egg mixture over chicken and vegetables. Top with remaining ½ cup cheese. Bake 30 to 35 minutes, or until set. Let quiche cool or 10 to 15 minutes before serving.

Menu: Cheesy Chicken and Asparagus Quiche

Spring Salad with Strawberries

Ingredients

1 lb. Salad greens, of choice
1 pt. fresh strawberries, sliced

Instructions

Mix salad greens and strawberries in a bowl. Add lemon-poppy seed dressing (to taste) and toss well. Top with sliced almonds and serve immediately. Serves 12.

Menu: Cheesy Chicken and Asparagus Quiche

SPECIALTIES

Lemon-Poppy Seed Dressing

Ingredients

Made 6 recipes
Zest and juice of 1 fresh lemon
⅓ cup rice vinegar (or mild
champagne vinegar or
strawberry/raspberry vinegar)
¼ cup sugar
½ cup vegetable oil
1 Tbs. poppy seeds
2 Tbs. sliced almonds, toasted
(for garnish)

Instructions

Mix zest and juice of lemon with vinegar. Add sugar and stir until sugar dissolves. Add oil and poppy seeds, and mix well. Refrigerate until ready to serve.

Dill Butter

Ingredients

¾ cup fresh dill weed
3 Tbs. fresh parsley leaves
2 sticks unsalted butter
1 Tbs. fresh lemon juice
¾ tsp. salt
⅛ tsp. cayenne

Instructions

Finely chop dill weed and parsley leaves in a food processor. Add butter and process until well combined. With the motor running, add lemon juice through the feed tube. Season with salt and cayenne. Yield: 1 cup butter.

Lemon Bisque

Ingredients

1 small pkg. Lemon Jell-O
Juice and rind of 1 lemon
1 large can evaporated milk
1 ¼ cups boiling water
1 cup sugar

Instructions

Dissolve Jell-O in water. Add sugar and lemon. Refrigerate about 30 minutes to start congealing (will be syrupy). Whip evaporated milk until stiff. Add Jell-O mixture to whipped milk. Pour over crumb crust below. Chill until firm.
Crust: 2 ½ cups vanilla wafer crumbs. Pour half of crumbs on bottom of 9 x 13" baking dish. Pour lemon Jell-O mixture over crumbs. Crumble rest of wafers on top. Refrigerate till chilled.

Menu: Cheesy Chicken and Asparagus Quiche

SPECIALTIES

Wild Rice Chowder Menu

Wild Rice Chowder with Ham

Wild Rice Chowder with Ham

Spinach Salad with Raspberry Vinaigrette

Poached Pears with Raspberry Sauce

Girls waiting for their Wild Rice Chowder

SPECIALTIES

Wild Rice Chowder with Ham

Ingredients

1 cup uncooked wild rice, rinsed
2 cups water
¼ cup butter or olive oil
1 cup chopped onions
3-6 garlic cloves, minced
½ cup flour
4 cups chicken broth
3 peeled, cubed potatoes
1 pkg. baby carrots
½ tsp. dried thyme leaves
½ tsp. nutmeg
⅛ tsp. pepper
1 (16 oz.) can whole kernel
corn, undrained
2 cups half and half
2 cups cubed ham

Instructions

In heavy saucepan, combine wild rice and water. Cover and bring to a boil. Lower heat and simmer for 30-45 minutes, until rice is tender. Do not drain. Set aside. In large stockpot, melt butter or heat olive oil. Add onions and garlic and sauté until tender. Add flour and cook, stirring constantly, for 1 minute. Stir in chicken broth and mix well. Add potatoes, carrots, and seasoning. Cover, bring to boil, and simmer 20-30 minutes until slightly thickened. Add corn (with its liquid). Cover and simmer an additional 20 minutes until vegetables are tender. Stir in half and half, ham and the cooked wild rice. Cook until steam, but do not boil. Serves 8-10.

(Optional: Substitute cubed ham or cooked chicken, or shrimp, or even try cooked meatballs - or no meat at all)

Menu: Wild Rice Chowder with Ham

SPECIALTIES

Spinach Salad with Raspberry Vinaigrette

Ingredients

2 lb. spinach, stemmed
½ cup thinly sliced red (Spanish) onion
½ cup thinly sliced mushrooms
¼ tsp. ground pepper
¼ cup sunflower seeds, toasted
Raspberry Vinaigrette (recipe follows)

Instructions

In a large bowl, combine the vinaigrette, spinach, onion, pepper, and half the sunflower seeds. Toss to coat the spinach with the dressing. To serve, divide among individual plates. Top each with an equal amount of the remaining sunflower seeds. Serves 8.

Raspberry Vinaigrette

Ingredients

⅓ cup thawed unsweetened apple juice concentrate
3 Tbs. raspberry vinegar
3 Tbs. water
2 Tbs. powdered fruit pectin
2 Tbs. olive oil
2 tsp. Dijon mustard
1 Tbs. chopped fresh thyme or
½ tsp. dried thyme
¼ tsp. ground pepper

Instructions

In a small bowl, combine the apple juice, vinegar, water, and pectin. Whisk until the pectin dissolves, about 1 minute. Add the olive oil, mustard, thyme, and pepper and whisk until blended. Refrigerate for at least 1 hour before using; the pectin will cause the dressing to thicken slightly as it chills.

Menu: Wild Rice Chowder with Ham

SPECIALTIES

Poached Pears with Raspberry Sauce

Ingredients

6 pears, slightly ripened
4 cups water
2 cups sugar
1 Tbs. fresh lemon juice
1 tsp. grated lemon rind
1 cinnamon stick
3 whole cloves
I inch or 2 of vanilla bean,
or use I Tbs. vanilla

Instructions

Peel the pears and drop in a bowl of water with a little lemon juice in it to keep the pears from discoloring. Bring above ingredients to a full rolling boil in a saucepan with very high sides. Add the pears and then cover and keep boiling until the pears are tender when stuck with a fork. This will probably take 30 minutes. When done they should be translucent. Cool in the juice, cover and refrigerate. They are better if they sit overnight. Serve masked in raspberry sauce.

Elberta peaches can be used just as well

Raspberry Sauce

Ingredients

1 (10 oz.) package frozen
raspberries
1 Tbs. fine sugar
1 Tbs. kirsch (optional)

Instructions

Thaw frozen raspberries and put through a blender or food processor. Whir until thickened. Strain through a sieve into a bowl and add sugar and kirsch, if desired. Cover and tightly refrigerate.

Menu: Wild Rice Chowder with Ham

POULTRY

Our Fathers didn't eat chicken – Why Should We?

That included southern fried or baked chicken and the proverbial holiday turkey. Dad didn't make an issue about it. He simply carried a piece of ham wrapped up in a paper napkin to the family Thanksgiving dinner, casually pulled it out of his coat pocket and plopped it on to his plate in lieu of the dead bird. However, if you are like the rest of the population, you will look forward to a well-prepared bird of any kind.

My Uncle Ed had fun being a wise guy. He would pull into the "Fat-Boy" drive-in curb service and order pheasant under glass. Surprisingly, they never had that on the menu and neither do we have a menu featuring pheasant under glass. Maybe we will in a future book.

Throughout my growing up years, chicken was a special Sunday dinner treat. Especially fried chicken. I remember when I was a small boy my grandmother going out back, grabbing a bird by the neck and proceeding to swing it into a vertical circle, ringing its neck. Then, it was released to run rampant around the back yard – like a chicken with its head cut off.

It wasn't just me who equated chicken with being well off! Which president prophesied a chicken in every American's pot? OK, here are the facts. It was attributed to Hoover, but Hoover never promised a chicken in every pot. It was part of a Republican Party campaign slogan regarding prosperity, relating that a chicken in every pot and a car in every garage had been made possible by the Harding-Coolidge Republican administration. My grandmother was a Republican. If the devil himself had been on the docket, she still would have voted a straight Republican ticket.

I never saw my grandmother wring a turkey's neck. I guess it's time to get out the hatchet to fulfill the Turkey Verde.

– Bill

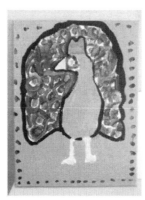

Black & white copy
of color original by
Ruby Wolter

POULTRY

Turkey Verde Menu

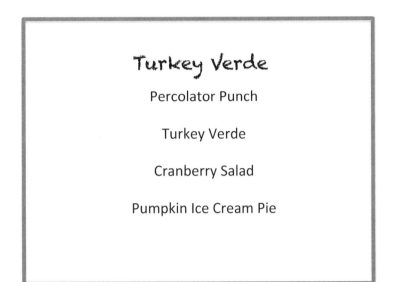

Turkey Verde

Percolator Punch

Turkey Verde

Cranberry Salad

Pumpkin Ice Cream Pie

Percolator Punch

Ingredients

2 qt. cranberry juice
2 qt. unsweetened pineapple juice
1 qt. water
⅔ cup light brown sugar
1 Tbs. whole cloves
1 Tbs. whole allspice
4 cinnamon sticks
1 lemon, quartered

Instructions

Combine juices and water in bottom of a 30 cups percolator. Place remaining ingredients in basket. Perk 20 minutes. Remove basket; serve hot. Yield: 30 cups.

Menu: Turkey Verde

POULTRY

Turkey Verde

Ingredients

2 to 3 bunches fresh
broccoli (3 lb.)
1 (12 oz.) pkg. egg noodles
2 Tbs. butter
1 (5 oz.) can water
chestnuts, drained and sliced
6 cups cooked turkey,
cut into bite-sized pieces
1 stick butter
1 cup toasted
slivered almonds
2 cups heated cream
¼-c. sherry (can omit)
Salt and white pepper
½ cup flour
Parmesan cheese

Instructions

Trim broccoli and blanch in boiling water for 5 minutes. Cool immediately under cold water, then drain well. Reserve some of the best broccoli florets for decoration; chop remaining broccoli coarsely.

Cook and drain noodles. Toss with 2 Tbs. butter and chestnuts.

Melt 1 stick butter in a saucepan over low heat. Mix in flour and continue stirring for 2 to 3 minutes. Whisk in cream and stir until sauce is thick. Add sherry and season to taste with salt and white pepper.

Preheat oven to 350°F. Place cooked noodles and water chestnuts in bottom of two buttered 9"x13" baking dishes. Spread chopped broccoli on top. Add a layer of turkey and spoon half the sauce over each dish. Decorate edges of casseroles with broccoli florets and sprinkle with almonds and cheese. Bake for 30 minutes. Serves 12 to 14. Can be frozen.

Menu: Turkey Verde

POULTRY

Cranberry Salad

Ingredients

1 pt. fresh cranberries
1 cup sugar
1 (8 oz.) can pineapple chunks, undrained
Orange or pineapple juice
1 (3 oz.) pkg. cherry, raspberry, or cranberry flavored gelatin powder
1 envelope unflavored gelatin
4 oranges, peeled, seeded
1 cup chopped pecans, chopped
Lettuce leaves
Garnishes: mayonnaise, paprika or grated dried cranberries

Instructions

Finely chop cranberries. Add sugar. Refrigerate ½ hour.Drain pineapple, reserving juice. Set pineapple aside. Add water or other additional orange or pineapple juice to reserved pineapple juice to equal 1 ¾ cups. Dissolve gelatins in juice mixture in a medium saucepan over low heat. Pour into a greased 13 x 9 x 2-inch baking dish or gelatin mold. Refrigerate. When gelatin begins to set, add cranberries, pineapple, oranges, and pecans. Refrigerate until congealed. Cut into squares or unmold, and serve on crisp lettuce leaves. Garnish, if desired. Serves 12.

Menu: Turkey Verde

Pumpkin Ice Cream Pie

Ingredients

2 cups canned pumpkin
2 tsp. cinnamon
¼ tsp. ginger
1 deep dish pie shell
24 oz. pecan ice cream
1 ½ tsp. nutmeg
½ tsp. ground cloves
1 cup pecans, whole

Instructions

Soften ice cream and mix in ingredients. Place into ginger snap or graham cracker pie shell. Freeze. Decorate with whipped cream and pecans when ready to serve. Serves 8.

Menu: Turkey Verde

POULTRY

Chicken Kiev Menu

Chicken Kiev with Parsley Butter

Chicken Kiev with Parsley Butter

Springtime Rice and Asparagus Salad

Marinated Carrots

Cherry Pound Cake with Frosting

Minted Fruit Toss

Chicken Kiev with Parsley Butter

Ingredients

¾ cup butter, melted and divided
½ cup fine dry bread crumbs
2 Tbs. grated Parmesan cheese
1 tsp. dried basil
1 tsp. dried oregano
½ tsp. garlic salt
¼ tsp. salt
4 boneless, skinless chicken breast halves
¼ cup chicken broth (or dry white wine)
¼ cup chopped green onions
¼ cup chopped fresh parsley

Instructions

Pour ¼ cup butter in large bowl. Combine breadcrumbs and the next 5 ingredients. Dip chick breasts in melted butter, and then coat with crumb mixture. Place chicken in an ungreased 2 qt. baking dish. Bake at 375°F. for 50 to 60 minutes or until chicken is tender. Add broth (wine), green onions, and parsley to remaining ½ cup butter. When chicken is golden brown, pour butter sauce over. Continue baking for 3 to 5 minutes more.

Menu: Chicken Kiev with Parsley Butter

POULTRY

Springtime Rice and Asparagus Salad

Ingredients

1 (14 ½ oz.) can chicken broth
1 cup long grain rice
10 oz. fresh asparagus cut into 2-inch pieces (about 2 cups)
¾ cup shelled fresh peas or frozen peas
¼ cup snipped fresh cilantro or parsley
3 green onions, sliced
4 Tbs. olive oil or salad oil
½ tsp. finely shredded lemon peel
3 Tbs. dairy sour cream or plain yogurt
¼ tsp. salt
¼ tsp. ground white pepper
Fresh spinach leaves
3 cups torn fresh spinach
Twisted lemon slices (optional)
3 Tbs. lemon juice
⅓ cup pecan halves or slivered almonds, toasted

Instructions

Add enough water (about ¼ cup) to broth to make 2 cups. In a saucepan bring broth to boiling. Add rice. Return to boiling; reduce heat. Cover; simmer about 15 minutes or until tender. Meanwhile, cook asparagus, covered, in a small amount of boiling water for 2 minutes. Add peas; cook 2 to 3 minutes more until crisp-tender. Drain. In large bowl combine cooled rice, asparagus and peas, cilantro or parsley, and onions. In small bowl combine oil, lemon peel, lemon juice, sour cream or yogurt, salt, and pepper. Pour over rice mixture; toss to coat. Cover; chill thoroughly. To serve, line a large platter with spinach leaves. Top with torn spinach, then rice mixture. Garnish with lemon slices, if desired, and toasted nuts.
(Prep. Time: 25 minutes)

Menu: Chicken Kiev with Parsley Butter

POULTRY

Marinated Carrots

Ingredients

2 lb. carrots,
cut in ½-inch slices
1 medium onion,
sliced in rings
1 (16 oz.) can tomato sauce
¼ cup vegetable oil
1 green pepper, sliced
¾ cup vinegar
1 cup granulated sugar
½ tsp. pepper
1 tsp. salt

Instructions

Cook carrots in water about 8 to 10 minutes; drain. Combine with remaining ingredients and marinate several hours or overnight. Stir occasionally. Serves 8-10.

In many cookbooks, this is called Copper Pennies.

Cherry Pound Cake with Frosting

Ingredients

1 ½ cups shortening OR 1 cup
shortening and ½ cup butter
3-¾ cup plain flour
6 eggs
¾ cup milk
½ tsp. almond
½ tsp. vanilla
3 cups sugar
1 small jar cherries (chopped/
drained)
FROSTING:
¼ cup margarine/butter
3 oz. cream cheese (room
temperature)
2 cups confectioners' sugar
1 tsp. vanilla
½ cup coconut (optional)
½ cup chopped nuts (optional)
1 small jar cherries, chopped/
drained

Instructions

Mix all ingredients. Bake in a well greased and floured tube pan at 300°F. for 2 hours. Start in cold oven. Let cool in pan 15 minutes.

Menu: Chicken Kiev with Parsley Butter

POULTRY

Minted Fruit Toss

Ingredients

¼ cup chopped fresh mint
¼ cup orange juice
3 Tbs. raspberry vinegar
3 Tbs. walnut or
vegetable oil
2 Tbs. honey
2 (16 ½ oz.) cans pitted Bing
cherries, drained
2 (11 oz.) can mandarin orange
sections, drained
2 apples, cubed
1 banana, sliced
4 kiwifruit, peeled and sliced
1 cup seedless green grapes

Menu: Chicken Kiev with Parsley Butter

Instructions

Stir together first 5 ingredients in a large bowl; add cherries and remaining ingredients, tossing to coat. Cover and chill 2 hours.
Yield: about 8 cups.

POULTRY

Smoked turkey Sandwich Menu

Smoked Turkey and Watercress Sandwiches

Smoked Turkey and Watercress Sandwiches
with Curried Apricot Mayonnaise

Fresh Pesto Pasta Salad

Watermelon Wedge

Crème De Menthe Brownie or Fresh Fruit Cups

Smoked Turkey and Watercress Sandwiches
Ingredients   Instructions

8 pita bread rounds, tortillas, etc.
1-½ lb. sliced smoked turkey
2 watercress bunches, trimmed (or any greens you choose)
8 plum tomatoes, sliced
1 cup walnuts, chopped (if desired)
Curried Apricot Mayonnaise

Preheat oven to 350°F. Place pita bread on baking sheet and heat in oven until just warm, about 5 minutes.
For a buffet: Cut rounds in half, forming pockets. Place in napkin-lined basket and keep warm. Arrange turkey, watercress and tomatoes on platter. Place walnuts and mayonnaise in bowls; allow diners to assemble their own sandwiches. YIELD: 8 servings.

with Curried Apricot Mayonnaise

Menu: Smoked Turkey and Watercress Sandwiches

POULTRY

Curried Apricot Mayonnaise

Ingredients

1-½ cups mayonnaise
¼ cup apricot jam (used Smuckers Simply 100% Fruit)
½ Tbs. curry powder

Instructions

Whisk ingredients in medium bowl to blend well. (Can be prepared 2 days ahead. Cover and refrigerate.) Makes about 1¾ cups.

Note: Can adjust this to taste. I used more Smuckers Simply 100% Fruit (apricot) than the recipe called for.

Fresh Pesto Pasta Salad

Ingredients

1 (16 oz.) package small shell pasta
⅓ cup red wine vinegar
1 Tbs. sugar
1 tsp. seasoned pepper
½ tsp. salt
1 tsp. Dijon mustard
1 garlic clove, pressed
¾ cup olive oil
1 cup chopped fresh basil
1 (3 oz.) package shredded Parmesan cheese
½ cup toasted pine nuts
Garnishes: gourmet mixed baby salad greens; grape tomatoes; small, yellow pear-shaped tomatoes

Instructions

PREPARE pasta according to package directions; drain. WHISK together vinegar and next 5 ingredients. Gradually whisk in olive oil. ADD vinaigrette to pasta. Add basil, cheese, and pine nuts; toss to combine. Garnish, if desired. Yield: 8 servings.

Menu: Smoked Turkey and Watercress Sandwiches

POULTRY

Crème De Menthe Brownie

Ingredients

Brownies:
1 cup sugar
½ cup butter, softened
1 cup flour
1 (16 oz.) can
Hershey's syrup
1 tsp. vanilla
4 eggs, well beaten
Mint Frosting:
2 cups powdered sugar
½ cup butter
Few drops green food coloring
2 Tbsp. milk
⅛-¼ tsp. peppermint
or mint extract
Glaze:
½ cup chocolate chips
3 Tbsp. butter

Instructions

Cream butter and sugar. Add all other ingredients and mix until thoroughly blended. Bake at 350°F. in a greased 9" x 13" pan for 20-25 minutes. Cool. Mint Frosting: Beat ingredients together until smooth. Frost cooled brownies. Glaze: Smooth over green frosting layer and refrigerate until set.

I often offer seasonal fresh fruit for dessert for those who avoid sugar.

Menu: Smoked Turkey and Watercress Sandwiches

POULTRY

Stuffed Turkey Breast Menu

Vegetable-Stuffed Turkey Breast

Vegetable-Stuffed Turkey Breast

Bean Bundles

Rice Pilaf

Stuffed Apple-Cinnamon Salad

Spicy Pumpkin Squares

POULTRY

Vegetable-Stuffed Turkey Breast

Ingredients

2 Tbs. margarine
1 cup chopped red onion
2 cups sliced mushrooms
1 cup shredded carrot
2 cups drained thawed frozen chopped spinach
2 Tbs. chopped fresh parsley
1 Tbs. grated Parmesan cheese
½ tsp. dried basil leaves
1 slice reduced-calorie white bread, finely chopped
1 cup low-sodium chicken broth
1 Tbs. grated lemon zest
One 2 lb., 13 oz. skinless boneless turkey breast (or skinless boneless chicken breasts)

Instructions

In large nonstick skillet, melt margarine over medium-high heat; add onion. Cook, stirring frequently, 4 minutes. Add mushrooms and carrot; cook, stirring frequently, 4-5 minutes, until tender. Stir in spinach, parsley, cheese and basil; cook 2 minutes. Remove from heat; stir in bread, 2 tablespoons of the broth and the lemon zest. Set aside. Preheat oven to 325°F. Spray a 13"x 9" baking pan with nonstick cooking spray. Arrange turkey between two sheets of plastic wrap; with meat mallet or rolling pin, pound turkey to even thickness. Remove top sheet of plastic wrap from turkey; spread mushroom mixture down center of turkey breast, leaving 2½" border on all sides. Starting with short side, roll turkey breast jelly-roll style to enclose filling. Secure roll at 2" intervals wit poultry string; arrange seam-side down in prepared pan. Pour remaining ¾ cup plus 2 tablespoons broth over turkey; cover with foil tent. Bake 1 to 1½ hours, basting frequently with broth, until meat thermometer inserted in center of roll reaches 180°F. Transfer turkey to carving board; let stand 10 minutes before slicing.

Menu: Vegetable-Stuffed Turkey Breast

POULTRY

Bean Bundles

Ingredients

Fresh green beans
Carrots
Red bell pepper

Instructions

Cook fresh green beans with carrot and red bell pepper strips in boiling water to cover until crisp-tender. Plunge into ice water to stop the cooking process; drain and set aside. Cook yellow squash in boiling water to cover until crisp-tender. Plunge into ice water to stop the cooking process, and drain. Cut squash into ½-inch-thick slices, and remove pulp from center of each slice with a round cutter or knife. Secure vegetables in bundles with squash rings, and place in a lightly greased 13 x 9-inch baking dish. Cover and chill 8 hours, if desired. Drizzle bean bundles with melted butter, and bake, covered, at 350F. for 20 to 25 minutes or until thoroughly heated.

Stuffed Apple-Cinnamon Salad

Ingredients

6 apples, cored and pared
1-½ cups sugar
2 cups water
½ cup red cinnamon candies
Red food coloring
2 pkg. cream cheese, softened
½ cup nuts, chopped

Instructions

Boil sugar, water, and candies to make a syrup. Add a few drops of food coloring. Cook apples slowly in syrup until transparent but not soft. Remove from syrup; drain and cool. Stuff with cream cheese nut mixture. Serve on crisp lettuce.

Menu: Vegetable-Stuffed Turkey Breast

POULTRY

Spicy Pumpkin Squares

Ingredients

1 (18 ½ oz.) pkg.
spice cake mix
½ cup margarine
or butter, softened
3 eggs
1 (16 oz.) can pumpkin
1 tsp. ground cinnamon
1 tsp. ground ginger
1 tsp. nutmeg
1 ¼ cups quick-cooking oats
¼ cup firmly packed
brown sugar
¼ cup chopped nuts
1 (14 oz.) can
Eagle Brand Milk
½ tsp. Salt

Instructions

In a large bowl, beat cake mix, oats, margarine, sugar and 1 egg until crumbly. Reserve 2 cups crumb mixture; press remainder firmly on bottom of 13" x 9" pan. Bake 15 minutes. Meanwhile, stir nuts into reserved crumb mixture; set aside. In large bowl, beat remaining ingredients until well blended. Spread evenly over prepared crust. Top with reserved crumb mixture. Bake 35 minutes or until golden brown. Cool. Serve warm or chilled with ice cream or whipped cream. Refrigerate leftovers.

Menu: Vegetable-Stuffed Turkey Breast

POULTRY

<u>Chicken Vieux Carre Menu</u>

Chicken Vieux Carre

Chicken Vieux Carre

Yellow Rice

New Wave Spinach Salad

Coca Roca Cloud Cake

Take a trip to New Orleans. The Vieux Carre is the oldest neighborhood in New Orleans. Most of us call it the French Quarter. The buildings present today reflect Spanish Colonial styles since they were build under Spanish rule. That was because two great fires in the late 1700's destroyed the French structures so the Spanish re-constructed according to their tastes. The results were flat tiled roofs, stucco siding and balconies with decorative ironwork. Much of the architecture was dictated by fire codes – commendable for the early 19th century. (No doubt, they had been burned before.)

Antique vase

We can skip the rest of the history until the 1920's when the unconventional art community moved in and started restoration. Now the Vieux Carre is an offical historic district.

With that brief background, try to create a vision of yourself with significant other casually relaxing on a balcony in the Vieux Carre, waiting to be served your dinner, "Chicken Vieux Carre." Bon Appétit!

POULTRY

Chicken Vieux Carre

Ingredients

12 large chicken breasts
2 tsp. salt, divided
½ tsp. freshly ground white pepper
½ tsp. paprika
5 Tbs. butter, margarine, bacon drippings, or olive oil
½ cup chopped fresh or frozen onion
½ cup chopped celery
2 cloves garlic, finely chopped or ¼ tsp. garlic powder
½ cup chopped fresh or frozen bell pepper.
1 (16 oz.) can peeled tomatoes
1 (12 oz.) can tomato juice
1 cup beef bouillon or white wine
1 Tbs. minced dried or fresh parsley
2 tsp. Worcestershire sauce
½ tsp. ground mace

Instructions

Skin chicken breasts and pat dry with paper towels. Sprinkle with 1 tsp. salt, white pepper, and paprika; sauté in butter. Cook over medium heat in a large iron skillet. When breasts are lightly golden on both sides remove from skillet to two 13- x 9- x 2-inch casseroles for prettiest arrangement. Sauté onion, celery, garlic, and bell pepper and cook about 15 minutes. Add tomatoes, tomato juice, beef bouillon or wine, and remaining 1 tsp. salt. Add parsley, Worcestershire sauce, and mace. Simmer sauce about 25 minutes, and then pour over chicken breasts. Cover casseroles tightly with foil. Bake in a preheated 375°F. oven for 1 hour. NOTE: To serve 6, reduce tomato juice and all other ingredients by half with the exception of the canned tomatoes and bouillon or wine. They remain the same.

Menu: Chicken Vieux Carre

POULTRY

New Wave Spinach Salad

Ingredients

Spinach
watercress
cubed Macintosh apples
cubed avocado
toasted pecans
pomegranate seeds (if available).

Instructions

Mix it, toss it and try it with the tangerine vinaigrette.

Menu: Chicken Vieux Carre

Tangerine Vinaigrette

Ingredients

1 Tbs. minced garlic
1 Tbs. minced shallots
¼ cup fresh orange juice
1 Tbs. grated orange zest
3 to 4 Tbs. grated lime juice
1 Tbs. grated lime zest
½ cup plus 2 Tbs.
tangerine juice
1 ½ Tbs. fresh lemon juice
2 Tbs. sugar
¾ cup extra-virgin olive oil

Instructions

Combine all the ingredients except the oil and whisk to blend and dissolve the sugar. Slowly whisk in the oil to emulsify and thicken.
NOTE: This is better if made a day before using. It will keep for up to 2 weeks in the refrigerator. Makes about 1 cup.

Menu: Chicken Vieux Carre

POULTRY

Coca Roca Cloud Cake

Ingredients

2 cups whipping cream
½ cup sweetened cocoa mix
1 (7 oz.) can Almond Roca candy
1 (10-inch) angel food cake

Instructions

Place the whipping cream in bowl of an electric mixer and whip on low speed. Slowly sprinkle in the cocoa mix and whip until stiff peaks form. Unwrap the candy and place it in a heavy plastic or paper bag. Put the candy in the freezer for 15 minutes. Roughly crush the candy with a hammer or mallet. Slice the cake in half to make 2 layers. Put about ¾ inch of the coca cream on the cut layer, and sprinkle generously with the crushed candy. Replace the top half and frost the cake with at least a ½-inch-thick coating of the cocoa cream. Press the remaining candy over the top and sides. Wrap lightly with plastic wrap and refrigerate for at least 4 hours before serving. For easier slicing, after the initial chilling, freeze the cake for at least 1 day. It will then slice like an ice cream cake.

Menu: Chicken Vieux Carre

POULTRY

Creamed Chicken Magnolia Menu

Creamed Chicken Magnolia in Puff Pastry

Tea Punch

Creamed Chicken Magnolia in Puff Pastry

Cold Asparagus
with Sesame Ginger Vinaigrette

Fruity Spinach Salad
with Honey Poppy Seed Dressing

Chocolate Lady Cake

Tea Punch

Ingredients

2 family-size tea bags
2 cups sugar
1 (12 oz.) can frozen
orange juice concentrate
1 (12 oz.) can frozen
lemonade concentrate
Sprigs of fresh mint

Instructions

Brew the tea using package directions. Pour into a 1 gal. container. Add the sugar, orange juice concentrate, lemonade concentrate and enough water to fill the container. Stir well. Serve over crushed ice. Garnish with mint sprigs. Yield: 1 gal..

Menu: Creamed Chicken Magnolia in Puff Pastry

POULTRY

Creamed Chicken Magnolia in Puff Pastry

Ingredients

Chicken Filling:
3 Tbs. butter
7 Tbs. flour
2 cups warm chicken broth
2 cups warm light cream or milk
Salt and pepper to taste
1 tsp. dry mustard
1 tsp. seasoned salt
½ tsp. paprika
¼ tsp. nutmeg
⅛ tsp. sugar
⅛ tsp. cayenne pepper
4 cups (about) chopped cooked chicken
1 (8 oz.) can sliced water chestnuts, drained
1 4 oz. jar pimentos
1 lb. mushrooms, optional
¼ cup cooking sherry or Madeira

Instructions

Melt the butter in a saucepan over medium heat. Blend in the flour until smooth. Add the broth and cream gradually, stirring constantly until smooth. Cook until thickened, stirring constantly. Add salt and pepper to taste, dry mustard, seasoned salt, paprika, nutmeg, sugar and cayenne pepper and mix well. Cook for 1 to 2 minutes, stirring constantly. Pour into the top of a large double boiler set over hot water. Fold in the chicken, water chestnuts, pimentos, and wine and mix gently. You may add 1 lb. sliced fresh mushrooms sautéed in butter or canned mushrooms, drained and sautéed. Keep warm until serving time. Pour into a large chafing dish. May serve chicken in patty shells for a luncheon. Serve in Chou Puffs or with Toast points. Makes 12 luncheon entrées or 100 cocktail buffet servings.

Cold Asparagus with Sesame Ginger Vinaigrette

Ingredients

1 lb. fresh asparagus, trimmed
Salt to taste
1 Tbs. toasted sesame seeds
1 small garlic clove
1 tsp. grated fresh gingerroot
2 Tbs. rice vinegar
2 Tbs. orange juice
2 tsp. soy sauce
2 Tbs. vegetable oil
1 Tbs. sugar
1 Tbs. hot chili oil
1 Tbs. sesame oil

Instructions

Cook the asparagus in lightly salted boiling water to cover in a medium skillet for 5 minutes or just until tender-crisp. Drain the asparagus and plunge into ice water to stop the cooking process. Drain and pat dry with paper towels. Arrange the asparagus on a serving platter. Combine the sesame seeds, garlic, gingerroot, vinegar, orange juice soy sauce, vegetable oil, sugar, chili oil and sesame oil in a blender and blend until thoroughly mixed. Pour the dressing evenly over the asparagus and serve. Yield: 4-6 servings

Menu: Creamed Chicken Magnolia in Puff Pastry

POULTRY

Fruity Spinach Salad with Honey Poppy Seed Dressing

Ingredients

½ cup low-fat mayonnaise
3 Tbs. honey
1 Tbs. lemon juice
1 Tbs. poppy seeds
1 pt. strawberries, quartered
1 (10 oz.) bag
pre-washed spinach,
torn into bite-size pieces
1 grapefruit, peeled, sectioned
and cut into bite-size pieces
2 Tbs. sunflower seeds

Instructions

Whisk the mayonnaise, honey, lemon juice and poppy seeds in a small bowl. Combine the strawberries, spinach and grapefruit in a large bowl. Add the dressing and toss to coat. Sprinkle with the sunflowers seeds just before serving.

Menu: Creamed Chicken Magnolia in Puff Pastry

Chocolate Lady Cake

Ingredients

2 (8 oz.) packages semisweet
chocolate chips
½ cup sugar, divided
¼ tsp. salt
½ cup hot water
4 eggs, separated
1 ½ tsp. vanilla
2 cups heavy cream, whipped
3 dozen ladyfingers
For garnish: shaved chocolate
and toffee bits

Instructions

Melt chocolate in top of double boiler. Add ¼ cup sugar, salt, and water. Cook, stirring constantly, until thickened. Add beaten egg yolks and cook 2 minutes. Stir in vanilla. Remove from heat; set aside. Beat egg whites until foamy. Gradually add remaining ¼ cup sugar and continue beating until stiff. Fold whites into chocolate mixture. Chill thoroughly; then fold in 1 cup whipped cream. Line springform pan with ladyfingers on bottom and sides. Pour half of mixture into pan. Add layer of ladyfingers, and top with remaining chocolate mixture. Chill 24 hours. Serve with 1 cup whipped cream on top and garnish with shaved chocolate and toffee bits. Yield: 12-16 servings.

Menu: Creamed Chicken Magnolia in Puff Past

GRAND OLE HOG

<u>**Hallelujah Ham Menu**</u>

Hallelujah Ham Loaves

Hallelujah Ham Loaves
(aka Ham Rolls)

Crunchy Garden Peas

Peach Salad

White Chocolate Lemon Curd Layer Cake

Descendants from the Eurasian Wild Boar? The next time we sit down to a pork roast or a ham sandwich, we should give thanks to our Maker for the ancestor of our meal, that is, the Eurasian Wild Boar. Yes, according to Oklahoma State University, you could be eating the descendant of the ancient wild boar.

If that isn't food for thought, (no pun intended), how would you like a once popular pig statuette from ancient Persia? –That's OK, neither would I.

The pig has been under development for domestication for as long as 12,000 years. My understanding is that a pig farm can be rather unpleasant to the olfactory system. Also, the transformation from livestock to grocery store packaged meat is not a pretty picture. So, I will choose to skip that part and go to the dinner table.

Let's discuss eating. When we eat the pig today, we are eating the domestic pig and generally we call it pork. "Pork" commonly denotes fresh pig meat as opposed to cured or smoked, after which it becomes ham or bacon. Fresh pork is a common ingredient in sausage.

Our menus include both ham and pork meats. Sausage shows up in some recipes but not in this section.

Turn on Handel's "Messiah" while preparing the next menu. Sing along. Have fun with your food!

– Bill

GRAND OLE HOG

Hallelujah Ham Loaves (aka Ham Rolls)

Ingredients

1 cup butter
2-3 Tbs. poppy seed
1 tsp. Worcestershire sauce
4 Tbs. prepared mustard
6 green onions, chopped
2 lb. honey ham, minced
12 oz. Swiss cheese, grated
8 oz. grated Parmesan cheese
12 oz. grated sharp cheddar
cheese
Rolls of your choice

Instructions

Preheat oven to 400°F. Cream butter, poppy seeds, Worcestershire sauce and mustard. Add ham, onion, and cheese; mix well. Split rolls in half lengthwise and place cut side up in pan. Spoon ham mixture on top. Cover with remaining halves. (You may seal and freeze at this point, if desired.) To bake, cover with foil. Bake 10 minutes or until heated thoroughly.

Out of this world if you make your own rolls. Great for parties!

Crunchy Garden Peas

Ingredients

1 16 oz. pkg. frozen petite
garden peas
1 4 oz. jar diced pimento
1 cup grated sharp cheddar
cheese
½ cup finely chopped celery
1 small onion
1 (2oz.) pkg. slivered
almonds
1 Tbs. of mayonnaise
Lettuce leaves

Instructions

Zap peas in microwave. In a medium bowl, combine all ingredients except mayonnaise and lettuce leaves. Toss ingredients with dressing. If available, Marsetti Slaw dressing is preferred. Cover and chill at least one hour before serving. Serves 8.

Peach Salad

Ingredients

1 cup miniature marshmallows
1 (15 ½ oz.) can crushed
pineapple
1 cup coconut
1 (8 oz.) carton sour cream
undrained
6-8 peaches, halved
Menu: Hallelujah Ham Loaves

Instructions

Combine marshmallows, pineapple, coconut and sour cream; mix well. Spoon into peach halves. Serve chilled. Yield: 6 to 8 servings.

GRAND OLE HOG

White Chocolate Layer Cake

Ingredients

⅓ cup butter
2 cups sugar
4 eggs, separated (room temperature)
4 oz. high quality white chocolate
1 tsp. vanilla
⅔ cups whole milk
2 ¾ cups cake flour
1 tsp. baking powder
¾ tsp. salt
Lemons for garnish
White Chocolate Cream Cheese Frosting:
9 oz. high quality white chocolate
12 oz. cream cheese, room temperature
1 ½ sticks unsalted butter, room temperature
1 ½ tsp. freshly squeezed lemon juice
FILLING:
Lemon curd – purchase or make your own

Instructions

Pre-heat oven to 350°F. Butter and flour three 9" cake pans. (If you must use a pan twice to bake the 3 layers, refrigerate the batter while the other layers are baking.) Melt 4 oz. of white chocolate with ½ cup of the heavy cream over a double boiler. Cool. Sift together the flour, baking powder, and salt. In a large bowl, cream together the butter with 1 cup of the sugar. Beat the mixture until it is fluffy and white. Beat in each egg yolk, one at a time. Stir the remaining heavy cream, milk, and vanilla into the white chocolate mixture. Alternately, add the dry ingredients and chocolate mixture to the butter bend, beating well. In a clean bowl, beat the egg whites to form soft peaks. Beating, add the remaining (1 cup) of sugar to the whites. Beat until stiff. Gently fold into the cake batter. Pour the cake batter into the pans. Bake for 25-30 minutes or until a skewer inserted into the middle of the cakes comes out clean. Cool for 10 minutes in the cake pans. Turn the cakes out onto a wire rack to cool completely. While the cake layers are baking, prepare the frosting. Melt 9 oz. of white chocolate over a double boiler. Beat the cream cheese and white chocolate until smooth. Add in the butter and lemon juice. Beat until light and smooth. Once the cake layers have cooled completely, place one of the layers onto a plate or platter. Spread a thing layer of the frosting onto the cake. Top this layer with lemon curd. Repeat this for the middle layer. For the top layer, do not top with lemon curd. Cover the cake with a thin layer of frosting. Chill. Once this layer has hardened a bit, generously cover the sides and top of the cake with the frosting. (This will prevent any crumbs or lemon curd from showing through the frosting.) Garnish the cake with fresh lemon slices, mint leaves, and a swirl of lemon curd. Or use your imagination!

Menu: Hallelujah Ham Loaves

GRAND OLE HOG

Baked Glazed Ham Menu

Baked Glazed Ham

Baked Glazed Ham

Sweet Potato Angel Biscuits

Deviled Eggs

Dilled Peas and Potatoes Vinaigrette

Fresh Fruit with Strawberry Sauce

Strawberry Delight

Baked Glazed Ham

Ingredients

2 Tbs. sugar
1 Tbs. paprika
1 Tbs. chili powder
1 tsp. ground cumin
¾ tsp. ground cinnamon
½ tsp. ground cloves
1 (8 lb) smoked fully cooked ham
half, trimmed
1 (12 oz.) can cola
soft drink
(can use sugar free drink)
1 (8 oz.) jar plum or apricot
preserves
(can use all-fruit or no sugar
products)
⅓ cup orange juice

Instructions

COMBINE first 6 ingredients. Score fat on ham in a diamond pattern. Sprinkle ham with sugar mixture, and place in a lightly greased shallow roasting pan. Pour cola into pan. BAKE, covered, at 325°F. for 1 hour. Uncover and bake 15 more minutes. STIR together preserves and orange juice. Spoon ¾ cup glaze over ham and bake 15 more minutes or until a meat thermometer inserted into thickest portion registers 140°F. Let stand 15 minutes before slicing. Serve with remaining glaze. Yield: 16 servings.

Menu: Baked Glazed Ham

GRAND OLE HOG

Sweet Potato Angel Biscuits

Ingredients

3 packages active dry yeast
¾ cup warm water (100 to 110)
7 ½ cups all-purpose flour
1 Tbs. baking powder
1 Tbs. salt
1 ½ cups sugar
1 ½ cups shortening
3 cups canned mashed sweet
potatoes

Instructions

COMBINE yeast and ¾ cup warm water in a 2 cups liquid measuring cups; let stand 5 minutes. STIR together flour and next 3 ingredients in a large bowl; cut in shortening with a pastry blender until mixture is crumbly. Stir in yeast mixture and sweet potatoes just until blended. TURN dough out onto a lightly floured surface, and knead until smooth and elastic (about 5 minutes). Place dough in a well-greased bowl, turning to grease top. Cover and chill 8 hours, if desired. ROLL dough to ½-inch thickness; cut with a 2-inch round cutter. Freeze up to 1 month, if desired. Thaw biscuits; place on ungreased baking sheets. Cover and let rise in a warm place (85°F.), free from drafts, 20 minutes, or until doubled in bulk. BAKE at 400 for 10 to 12 minutes or until lightly browned. Yield: 7½ dozen.

Menu: Baked Glazed Ham

Deviled Eggs

Ingredients

12 large hard-cooked eggs
4 ½ Tbs. mayonnaise
1 ½ Tbs. Dijon mustard
1 tsp. Worcestershire sauce
3 dashes hot sauce, or to taste
Paprika
Salt, white pepper to taste

Instructions

Discard shells from eggs and slice each egg in half lengthwise. Remove yolks and arrange whites on a plate.In a bowl mash yolks with mayonnaise, mustard, hot sauce, and salt and pepper to taste and spoon mixture into whites. Chill deviled eggs, covered, 1 hour. Just before serving sprinkle eggs with paprika and serve cold.Makes 24 deviled eggs.

Menu: Baked Glazed Ham

GRAND OLE HOG

Dilled Peas and Potatoes Vinaigrette

Ingredients

8 small red potatoes (about 1 ½ lb.)
1 lb. sugar snap peas*
½ cup olive oil
6 Tbs. white wine vinegar
2 Tbs. minced fresh dill
½ tsp. salt
½ tsp. fresh ground pepper
6 green onions, chopped

Instructions

Cook potatoes in a Dutch oven in boiling water to cover 25 to 30 minutes or until tender; drain. Thinly slice. Cook snap peas in boiling water 2 minutes or until crisp-tender; drain. Plunge peas into ice water to stop the cooking process; drain. Whisk together oil and next 4 ingredients in a large bowl. Add sliced potatoes, snap peas, and onions, tossing gently to coat. Cover and chill 2 hours, or serve immediately. Yield: 6 to 8 servings.

*Substitute 1 (16 oz.) pkg. frozen sugar snap peas for fresh, if fresh peas are not available.

Menu: Baked Glazed Ham

Fresh Fruit with Strawberry Sauce

Ingredients

1 cup frozen unsweetened whole strawberries, thawed
2 tsp. sugar
¼ tsp. grated orange rind
2 cups orange sections (about 6 oranges)
1 cup cubed peeled kiwifruit (about 3 kiwifruit)

Instructions

Place the first 3 ingredients in a blender, and process until smooth; set sauce aside. Spoon ½ cup orange sections and ¼ cup kiwifruit into each of 4 small bowls; top each serving with 3 Tbs. sauce. Yield: 4 servings.

Menu: Baked Glazed Ham

GRAND OLE HOG

Strawberry Delight

Ingredients

CRUST:
1 cup all-purpose flour
¼ cup firmly packed
brown sugar
½ cup melted butter
½ cup chopped pecans
FILLING:
1 (10 oz.) pkg. frozen
strawberries, thawed, or 1 ½
cups sliced fresh strawberries
1 cup sugar
2 tsp. freshly squeezed lemon
juice
2 egg whites
½ pt. whipping
cream, whipped

Instructions

Combine flour, brown sugar, pecans, and butter. Bake at 350°F. for 20 minutes in a 9-inch square pan. Let cool. Combine strawberries, sugar, lemon juice, and egg whites; beat at high speed of electric mixer about 20 minutes or till light and fluffy. Fold whipped cream into strawberry mixture. Remove ⅓ of crumb mixture from pan; pat remaining crumbs into smooth layer. Pour strawberry mixture over crumbs in pan and sprinkle reserved crumbs over top; freeze.

Are you tired of strawberries? Try some other fruits in this recipe, (peaches, blueberries, mangos, others).

Menu: Baked Glazed Ham

GRAND OLE HOG

Tuscan Pork Loin

Tuscan Pork Loin

Tuscan Pork Loin
Rosemary Roasted Red-Bliss Potatoes
Green Beans Supreme
Rolls/Butter
Super Moist Blackberry Jam Cake with Caramel Icing

Imagine winter trees in Tuscany

GRAND OLE HOG

Tuscan Pork Loin

Ingredients

1 (4 lb.) boneless pork loin roast
1 (8 oz.) pkg. cream cheese, softened
1 Tbs. dried pesto seasoning
½ cup loosely packed fresh spinach leaves
6 bacon slices, cooked and drained
½ (12 oz.) jar roasted red bell peppers, drained
1 tsp. salt
1 tsp. paprika
½ tsp. pepper
Fresh spinach leaves

Instructions

Slice pork lengthwise, cutting down center, to but not through other side. Open halves, and cut down center of each half, cutting to but not through other sides. Open into a rectangle. Place plastic wrap over pork and pound to an even thickness with a meat mallet or rolling pin.

Spread cream cheese evenly down center of pork lengthwise. Sprinkle cream cheese evenly with dried pesto seasoning.

Arrange spinach over cream cheese, and top with bacon and red peppers.

Roll up pork starting with 1 long side. Secure at 2-inch intervals with kitchen string. Rub pork roll with salt, paprika, and pepper. Place, seam side down, on a lightly greased rack on an aluminum foil-lined pan.

Bake at 425°F. for 30 minutes or until a meat thermometer inserted into thickest portion registers 155°F. Remove from oven. Let stand 10 minutes.

Remove string from pork; cut into 1/2-inch-thick slices. Serve pork slices on a bed of fresh spinach leaves.

Menu: Tuscan Pork Loin

GRAND OLE HOG

Rosemary Roasted Red-Bliss Potatoes

Ingredients

3 lb. new potatoes
3 Tbs. olive oil
2 tsp. dried rosemary
1 tsp. garlic powder
½ tsp. tarragon
½ tsp. kosher salt
½ tsp. ground black pepper

Instructions

Preheat oven to 400°F. Wash potatoes, cut into halves or quarters, and place in a large bowl. In a small bowl, combine olive oil and seasonings. Pour over potatoes and toss to coat. Spread potatoes on roasting pan or rimed baking sheet. Bake for 40 to 45 minutes, or until potatoes are fork tender.

Yield: 6 to 8 servings.

Menu: Tuscan Pork Loin

Green Beans Supreme

Ingredients

3 (16 ounce) cans
French-style green beans, drained
1 (10½ oz.) can beef consommé
1 (4 oz.) can sliced mushrooms and liquid
½ cup butter, sliced
2 tsp. Maggi's seasoning
1 tsp. salt
½ tsp. seasoned salt
1 tsp. soy sauce

Instructions

Combine all ingredients in casserole (can be put into bundles). Bake at 325°F. degrees for 45 minutes. May be prepared 2 days ahead, then cooked when needed. Serves 10-12.

Menu: Tuscan Pork Loin

GRAND OLE HOG

Super Moist Blackberry Jam Cake

Ingredients

1 cup butter or margarine
2 cups sugar
6 eggs
2 cups seedless blackberry jam
3 cups sifted all-purpose flour
1 tsp. soda
1 tsp. cinnamon
1 tsp. cloves
1 tsp. allspice
½ cup buttermilk

Easy Caramel Icing:

½ cup butter
1 cup light brown sugar, packed
¼ cup light cream or evaporated milk
1 ¾ - 2 cups sifted confectioner's sugar

Menu: Tuscan Pork Loin

Instructions

Preheat oven to 325°F. Cream butter and sugar and beat until light and fluffy. Add eggs two at a time. Continue mixing after each addition. Add jam and beat well. Sift dry ingredients and add alternately with buttermilk. Pour into greased and floured 9" x 13" pan and bake for approximately 50 minutes to one hour. Spread top of cooled cake with caramel icing.

Easy Caramel Icing:

Melt ½ cup butter. Add 1 cup light brown sugar, packed. Boil over low heat for 2 minutes, stirring constantly. Stir in ¼ cup milk. Stir until it comes to a boil. Cool to lukewarm. Gradually add 1 ¾ to 2 cups sifted confectioner's sugar. Beat until spreading consistency. If icing becomes too stiff, add a little hot water.

GRAND OLE HOG

Rollup Ham Menu

Rollup Ham & Apparagus

Ham and Asparagus Rollups

Carrot with Dill

Fresh Spinach & Strawberries

Basil Batter Rolls

Banana Split Delight

"For gourmet food is where you find it and connoisseurs of the culinary art are found wherever there is good food," A Treasury of Great Recipes, Mary and Vincent Price.

GRAND OLE HOG

Ham and Asparagus Rollups

Ingredients

8 rectangular slices boiled ham
8 slices Swiss cheese
2 (10 oz.) packages asparagus spears, cooked and drained
1 Tbs. butter or margarine
1 Tbs. flour
¼ tsp. salt
1 Tbs. prepared horseradish
2 tsp. prepared mustard
½ tsp. Worcestershire sauce
½ tsp. grated onion
2 egg yolks, beaten
1 cup pineapple juice
½ cup milk

Instructions

Preheat oven to 350F. Place one slice of cheese on each slice of ham; top with 1 to 2 spears of asparagus. In medium sauce pan melt butter; blend in flour, salt, horseradish, mustard, Worcestershire and onion. Combine eggYolks and pineapple juice; gently stir into butter mixture. Stir in milk; cook over low heat, stirring constantly until thick and bubbling. Spoon one Tbs. of sauce over asparagus; roll ham and cheese around broccoli and secure with a toothpick. Place roll-ups in baking dish; cover and cook at 350F. for 25 to 30 minutes. Spoon any remaining hot mustard sauce over ham rolls just before serving. Yield: 6 to 8 servings.

Menu: Rollup Ham & Apparagus

GRAND OLE HOG

Carrot with Dill

Ingredients

8 carrots, grated
2 tablespoons dill
1½ tablespoons sesame oil
Salt and pepper to taste
Juice of 4 oranges
Orange zest, to taste
¼ cup chopped parsley

Instructions

Mix all the ingredients together in a large bowl.
Serves 8.

Fresh Spinach & Strawberries

Ingredients

1 lb. fresh spinach, washed and dried
1 pt. fresh strawberries
¾ cup sliced almonds, toasted
Poppy Seed Dressing

Instructions

Toss spinach and strawberries. Pour dressing over salad, then top with toasted almonds.

Menu: Rollup Ham & Apparagus

Lynn Wolter

GRAND OLE HOG

Basil Batter Rolls

Ingredients

2 packages active dry yeast
1 ½ cups warm water
(105° to 115°F.)
⅓ cup shortening
4 cups unbleached flour,
divided
¼ cup sugar
1 ½ tsp. salt
1 larger egg
2 Tbs. pesto
2 cloves garlic, minced
Cooking spray
Melted butter or margarine
(optional)

Instructions

Combine yeast and warm water in a 2 cups liquid measuring cut; let stand 5 minutes. Combine yeast mixture, shortening, 2 cups flour, and next 3 ingredients in a large mixing bowl; beat at medium speed with an electric mixer until well blended. Stir in pesto and garlic. Gradually stir in enough remaining flour to make a soft dough. (Dough will be sticky.) Cover and let rise in a warm place (85°F.), free from drafts, 50 minutes or until doubled in bulkStir dough; spoon into greased muffin pans, filling half full. Spray roll tops with cooking spray; cover and let rise in a warm place, free from drafts, 45 minutes. Bake at 375°F. for 15 minutes or until golden. Brush with melted butter if desired. Yield: 18 rolls.

Menu: Rollup Ham & Apparagus

GRAND OLE HOG

Banana Split Delight

Ingredients

SAUCE:
2 cups powdered sugar
12 oz. Can evaporated milk
½ cup margarine or butter
¾ cup chocolate chips

BASE:
24 creme-filled chocolate
sandwich cookies,
finely crushed (2 ¼ cups)
¼ cup melted butter

FILLING:
3 medium bananas,
thinly sliced
½ gal. vanilla ice cream,
softened
8 oz. can crushed pineapple,
drained
Whipped cream or topping
Chopped pecans, if desired
Maraschino cherries, if desired

Menu: Rollup Ham & Apparagus

Instructions

In medium saucepan, combine sauce ingredients; bring to a boil over medium-low heat. Cook 8 minutes, stirring constantly. Cool at least 45 minutes.In large bowl, combine cookie crumbs and margarine; mix well. Press lightly in bottom of ungreased 13x9-inch pan. Arrange sliced bananas over crumbs. Spoon half of ice cream over bananas; refrigerate remaining ice cream. Spoon half of cooled chocolate sauce over ice cream layer; freeze until firm. Spoon remaining ice cream over sauce layer. Spoon pineapple over ice cream. Cover; freeze until firm.To serve, cut into squares. Serve with remaining chocolate sauce and whipped cream; garnish with pecans and cherries. Yield: 24 servings.

Use Semi-sweet or dark chocolate chips.

What to include in a subject index is a good question. Generic type of food? Specific name of food? How about both? We tried to make this cross-reference as useful as we could. I hope you find it helpful.

Subject	Recipe	
almonds		
	Almond-Butter Cake	36
	Apple-Almond Cheesecake	45
	Turkey Verde	105
angel food cake		
	Cherries in the Snow	6
appetizer		
	Black-Eyed Pea Dip with Pita Chips	52
apple		
	Apple Cider Vinaigrette	41
	Apple Crisp	90
	Apple Enchiladas	23
	Apple-Almond Cheesecake	45
	Ham Cornets with Apple Horseradish Filling	58
	Stuffed Apple-Cinnamon Salad	116
apricot		
	Curried Apricot Mayonnaise	112
artichoke		
	Crab-Artichoke Tarts	59
	Rice and Artichoke Pie	88
	Roasted Red Pepper, Artichoke and Black Olive Dip	68
asparagus		
	Asparagus with Dill Sauce	13
	Cheesy Chicken and Asparagus Quiche	97
	Cold Asparagus with Sesame Ginger Vinaigrette	123
	Ham and Asparagus Rollups	137
	Springtime Rice and Asparagus Salad	108
aspic		
	Tomato Aspic with Cucumber	57
bacon		
	Brown Derby Cobb Salad	78
	Tuscan Pork Loin	133
banana split		
	Banana Split Delight	140
barbecue shrimp		

SUBJECT INDEX

SUBJECT INDEX

SUBJECT INDEX

SUBJECT INDEX

SUBJECT INDEX

SUBJECT INDEX

SUBJECT INDEX

SUBJECT INDEX

SUBJECT INDEX

SOURCES

Recipes come from various sources and they get "tweaked" and altered to suit the taste. Lynn is an experimenter and employs tactics such as trial and error to get the right ingredients and proportions. We honestly do not know or remember where many of the recipes were brought to Lynn's attention. There are some known starting references, however, that are acknowledged in these final pages.

SOURCES

SOURCES

SOURCES

Recipe		Source
Ham Cornets with Apple Horseradish Filling	58	Gourmet, June 1986
Hawaiian Delight	81	Cooking Light Magazine
Italian Love Cake	74	Lynn Wolter
Italian Pan Rolls	4	*Unknown*
Lemon Bisque	98	**Entertaining with Food and Flair**
Lemon Ice Box Pie	86	**Recipes from Miss Daisy's**
Lemon-Poppy Seed Dressing	98	**Culinary Memories of Merridun**
Little Bitty Cakes	61	Southern Living Magazine, June 1998
Mahogany Chicken	31	Lynn Wolter. A family favorite for almost thirty years!
Mandarin Spinach Salad with French Dressing	89	**Tea-Time at the Masters**
Margarita Strawberry Dessert	28	**Par 3: Tea-Time at the MASTERS**
Marinated Carrots	109	Lynn Wolter
Marinated Chicken with Vegetables	17	Southern Living Magazine, March 2000
Marinated Green Beans and Roasted Red Peppers	93	Bon Appetite Magazine, December 1998
Marinated Vegetables with Garlic and Thyme	47	Lynn Wolter
Mexican Cornbread	23	Mary Hemphill, Black Mountain, NC
Minted Fruit Toss	110	Southern Living Magazine
Mixed Grain Salad with Dried Fruit	44	Bon Appétit Magazine, August 1996
Mocha Tartlets	61	Gourmet, December 2001
Molasses Cookie Baskets	79	Bon Appétit Magazine, August 1992
New Wave Spinach Salad	120	**Cooking for Company**
No-Fuss Blue Cheese and Pear Salad	53	Better Homes and Gardens magazine, December 2005
Paella Salad	76	**Winston-Salem Heritage of Hospitality**
Passion Fruit Tartlets	62	http://www.foodtv.com
Passion Fruit Vinaigrette	30	**The Hali'imaile General Store Cookbook**
Peach Iced Tea	92	Southern Living Magazine, August 2003
Peach Salad	126	Lynn Wolter
Percolator Punch	104	**Heart of the Mountains**
Poached Pears with Raspberry Sauce	102	**The Mount Vernon Cookbook**
Pork Tenderloin with Cranberry-Orange Relish	38	Cooking Light, December 1996
Potato Salad	65	Lynn Wolter

SOURCES

SOURCES

Recipe		Source
Spinach Salad with Tarragon Vinaigrette	35	**Food for Thought**
Spring Salad with Strawberries	97	**Culinary Memories of Merridun**
Springtime Rice and Asparagus Salad	108	Lynn Wolter
St. Patrick's Day Cake	10	Lynn Wolter
Strawberry Delight	131	Lynn Wolter
Strawberry Dressing	83	Lynn Wolter
Stuffed Apple-Cinnamon Salad	116	Lynn Wolter
Stuffing Stuffed Mushrooms	47	Lynn Wolter
Summer Fruit Salad with Blueberry Vinaigrette	94	Lynn Wolter
Sunny Spring Lemonade	82	Lynn Wolter
Super Moist Blackberry Jam Cake'	135	Lynn Wolter
Sweet Potato Angel Biscuits	129	Southern Living Magazine, Feb 2001
Tangerine Vinaigrette	120	**Cooking for Company**
Tarragon Vinaigrette	35	**Food For Thought**
Tea Punch	122	Lynn Wolter
Tijuana-Caesar Salad	27	**Betty Crocker Celebrate!**
Tomato Aspic with Cucumber	57	**A Tea for All Seasons**
Tres Leches Cake	57	Lynn Wolter
Tuna Salad with Green Peppercorn Dressing	8	**In Chelsea's Kitchen**
Turkey Verde	105	**The Seasons of Big Thursday**
Tuscan Pork Loin	133	Southern Living Magazine, December 2005
Vegetable-Stuffed Turkey Breast	115	*Unknown*
Warm Blackberry Pie Sundaes	95	Lynn Wolter
White Chocolate Layer Cake	127	Lynn Wolter
Wild and Brown Rice Pilaf	39	Bon Appétit Magazine, November 2002
Wild Rice Chowder with Ham	100	http://busycooke.about.com
Yogurt Dill Dip	100	**Party Receipts** From The Charleston Junior League
You Can't beat a Good Pound Cake	100	Lynn Wolter
Zucchini Cup with Peas	40	Bon Appétit Magazine, December 1985

ABOUT THE AUTHOR

Lynn is an event coordinator for Northshore Baptist Church located on the east side of Lake Washington in the Seattle metro area. There, for the past 13 years, she has delighted about 100 monthly guests with a sit-down luncheon, never repeating a menu.

In the mountain region of western North Carolina, Lynn grew up in the town of Black Mountain. She graduated in Business at Meredith College in Raleigh, NC.

Living and traveling to many spots in the United States and 6 continents on the globe, Lynn gathered recipes and cooking techniques from every stop.

Delicious food preparation and hospitality has been her passion and she would like the readers of this book to become its users and enjoy the pleasures of a delicious meal.

Lynn still lives with her (first) husband, Bill, even after they jointly assembled this book and in spite of Bill's commentaries and fun facts scattered throughout.

Made in the USA
San Bernardino, CA
01 May 2013